101
WAYS TO DIE WITH A HORSE

LIVE
HAPPILY
EVER AFTER

An Essential Safety Guide
for Horse & Rider

by Tanya Buck

Illustrated by Jennipher Cunningham

101 Ways to Die With A Horse or Live Happily Ever After
An Essential Safety Guide
for Horse & Rider

Written by Tanya Buck
Illustrated by Jennipher Cunningham
Edited by Tom Locke • www.TomsTouchMemories.com
Graphic design by Hancey Design • www.HanceyDesign.com

Cataloging-in-Publication Data
Buck, Tanya
101 Ways to Die With A Horse or Live Happily Ever After
Library of Congress Control Number: 2016958637
I. Equine Safety Guide II. Horse and Rider III. Happily Ever After
IV. Groundwork V. Training
I.Tanya Buck
II. 101 Ways to Die With A Horse or Live Happily Ever After
ISBN 978-0692802458 Hdk

Printed in the United States
By Flying Frog

For my husband—it's likely this
book would never have come
to be without him.

TABLE OF
CONTENTS

INTRODUCTION

So you or someone you love wants to enter the horse world and become an equestrian. Or maybe you are returning to the horse world after many years. Or perhaps you have had horses for many years, but it seems accidents keep happening and the injury list and trips to the emergency room are adding up.

Now what?

Whether you, your child, or your spouse is the new equestrian in your household or you're a long-term horse owner, the fact is that the world of large, flighty, 1,100 pound, fear-based animals can be a bit daunting for all involved, and safety is the main concern—especially when starting out. How do you know what to do, how to act, when to do things like call the vet out, or even how to purchase a horse or saddle? What should you wear when in the presence of a horse? What does a horse eat, and where should he live? Do you need a trainer, and how do you find a good one if you do?

So many questions! And though no one book, video, or lesson can cover every safety contingency, *101 Ways to Die with a Horse or Live Happily Ever* will go over 101 of the most common and most important safety concerns and how to keep both you and your horse alive while you learn the equine way of thinking. This book is not intended to conclusively cover everything that can go wrong, but each death tip should help you understand how best to keep you and your horse happy and intact. The longer you ride and the more time you spend in the company of horses, the more you learn and the more comfortable you become.

Some long-term horse owners regularly do things incorrectly, and yet they live to tell about it. This doesn't mean you, possibly a newbie to the equine world, should follow their example. It's kind of like wearing a seat belt—it may not be a law around the world, yet we know it's generally safer to do it. The choice is ultimately yours regarding how you treat your horse and yourself, but keeping your horse safe will also keep you safe—whether on the ground, at the barn, or in the saddle.

May you have many safe horse-related hours ahead of you, and I wish you an abundance of happy trails!

PART I

SAFETY AT THE BARN

THE *Myth*

Your horse views the world through your eyes—using logic and common sense. He has no reason to fear anything as mundane as a plastic grocery bag blowing across the road. He should just go anywhere you want, and you shouldn't have to worry or think about a thing.

Happily EVER AFTER

Horses are reactive prey animals that have evolved to stay in a herd, reacting to everything in order to survive. Even though we have domesticated them, they are, by nature, fear-driven creatures. A horse's fear reaction is instantaneous and results in an immediate escape from the unknown. He doesn't think first; he reacts.

There is no way to train a horse to not be afraid, but you can teach him to control his emotions and to look to you as his safety net and protector until he gains more self-confidence in his everyday world. We must override the horse's genetics and be good leaders—trustworthy, fair, and consistent. Once he knows you are a safe haven, his confidence and trust in you will increase while his explosive reactions to fearful places and things will diminish.

A horse (and humans too) can only exist in one emotional state at a time, and there are only two to choose from: *trust* and *fear*. All other emotions fall tidily under one of these two categories.

There is no way to train a horse to not be afraid, but you can teach him to control his emotions and to look to you as his safety net and protector until he gains more self-confidence in his everyday world.

Your job is to keep your horse in the *trust* column. When he jumps the line and falls into *fear*, it is up to you to help bring him back to trust. To do this, understanding how your horse feels and thinks is most helpful in allowing you to choose the best way to help him.

For example, if he is afraid of a plastic bag blowing in his direction, one rider-reaction would be to keep his nose facing it so he has time to identify the object. This exercise also allows you time to gather yourself, soften your lower back, shorten your reins and then continue on your ride.

Sometimes a horse's reaction to some unseen thing is instantaneous and the best thing to do is to simply hang on tight until you can get him stopped. To avoid this, be aware at all times, and learn to watch the world through your horse's eyes. Help your horse trust you by being a good leader—someone he follows because he wants to, not because he feels he must. Keeping your horse safe will keep you safe; it is that simple.

TIDBIT
Horses have basically only two categories of objects to fear—things that move and things that don't.

DEATH TIP

2

▼

Demanding Respect Is The Best Way To Get It From Your Horse.

THE *Myth*

Your horse's respect for you is mandatory. To ensure he respects you, always act in a businesslike manner when you are with your horse. No laughing, no hugging or kissing him, and definitely do not allow him to rub his nose against you. Treat him like a piece of equipment rather than a living, breathing, feeling being. Demand that he be the perfect robotic horse in all circumstances. That way, you'll be safe.

Happily EVER AFTER

Horses are thinking, feeling beings, and we need to earn their respect rather than demand they submit by using fear tactics. Horses thrive and work hardest for us when they feel an affinity toward us and bond with us. They need to understand on both intellectual and emotional levels that doing what we want is beneficial to them. It's a fine line, this act of keeping the respect of your horse and having the feeling of camaraderie between the two of you.

It is as dangerous for the horse to have no respect for you as for the horse to 'respect' that which is only driven by fear—such as a plastic bag at the end of a stick.

In other words, it goes back to the same thing as always—the horse must feel safe. If he feels anything other than safe, he has crossed over into fear. And that is what can get you badly hurt.

Respect is not the attitude to strive for; it's better to look for and foster an understanding of the boundaries you want your horse to understand.

You must allow the horse to do what you permit and desire. The easiest and fastest way to gain his respect is by consistent, calm, and quiet repetition of each lesson you teach him. A horse begins to understand what you want in the first three to seven times he sees a new cue. By the tenth time you repeat the exact same thing, he has to look for your happy praise. Around the twenty-fifth repetition, he begins to respond to the cue in a methodical manner; again, he looks for affirmation from you, his trainer, telling him he did it right. After 101 times of doing as you ask within one second, the horse has learned the cue, and the behavior is trained.

Respect is not the attitude to strive for; it's better to look for and foster an understanding of the boundaries you want your horse to understand.

THE *Myth*

No need to know your horse's vital signs or how to take them. Why bother, isn't that what vets are for?

Happily EVER AFTER

Each animal is different, and by knowing your horse's normal vital signs, you may help save his in the event of an emergency.

Temperature is best taken rectally, so be safe and stand to the side of the horse, lifting his tail sideways, away from you. Gently insert a pre-lubricated (use saliva or Vaseline™) digital thermometer into the rectum, angling the tip slightly toward his front feet. Clean it when you are finished to avoid inadvertently spreading any disease.

The pulse (resting heart rate) can be taken using a stethoscope or your fingers. Find an artery at the inside of the jaw, under the tail at the tail bone or at the side of the horse's foot. You can also place your hand on the left side of the chest, just under the elbow; you will be able to feel the heart's beat. If using a stethoscope, the sound of lub-dub is one beat, and you must measure for a full minute. Anything over 40 beats per minute at rest is cause for concern.

> Knowing the horse's vital signs may well save his life in the event of an emergency.

VITAL SIGNS

TEMPERATURE
A horse's normal body temperature is 101.5° F (+ or −1°).

PULSE
The normal pulse rate is 36 to 42 beats per minute.

RESPIRATION
The normal resting rate is between 8-12 breaths per minute.

CAPILLARY REFILL TIME
The time it takes for color to return to gum tissue adjacent to teeth after pressing and releasing with your thumb—this is 1-2 seconds.

Respiration rate is the number of times your horse breathes per minute. Normal is about ten breaths per minute at rest. Watching his nostrils or flanks move in and out as he breathes and counting each cycle is the easiest way to know his respiration.

Capillary refill is the time it takes for color to return to his gums after you've pressed long enough to leave a white dot with your thumb. Normal is 1-2 seconds; any longer indicates he is dehydrated.

THE *Myth*

Common knowledge dictates you have three seconds to punish your horse. So, if your horse misbehaves (you can tell he did it on purpose because he has "that look," and, besides, he knows better), be sure to get after him immediately and punish him harshly. The best way is to yell at him at the top of your lungs and, if possible, take a swing at him.

Happily EVER AFTER

It's normal for horses (and people) to step out of bounds or to act up, but a horse's motivation is different from a human's. He doesn't stand out in his corral pondering how to get the best of you or how to take over being "the boss" of you. He is a horse, and his greatest ambition of the day is to eat what is in front of him and then maybe eat his buddy's food too.

If he behaves badly, your first reaction may be anger; that's normal. But showing your anger to your horse doesn't translate into immediate positive changes in him. The horse doesn't think, "Gee, she is really mad; I'd better straighten up and act right." Nope. Rather, he will react to the emotional outburst the way a horse reacts to anything he doesn't understand. His brain is not engaged, and he goes into reaction mode—which is to keep himself safe, usually by jumping, spinning, or running. Nothing else matters.

> ♘
>
> **You must find the reason for his behavior and your anger. What did you do, or not do, that allowed him the chance to step out of line?**

You must find the reason for his behavior and your anger. What did you do, or not do, that allowed him the chance to step out of line? Ask yourself if your first priority—to keep him safe—has been met. Was your attention on him so you knew his emotional state? If the unwanted behavior was your fault—and face it, it usually is—the fix is easy, because you simply change your outlook and actions.

Screaming and waving your arms will not make the horse want to follow and trust you. If you must reprimand a horse for something he does wrong, you must do so immediately—you don't have three full seconds, and you must do so in a way he understands—quietly, consistently, and without anger. Your goal is to correct the wrong, not scare the daylights out of him.

Your being angry enough to want to hurt your horse is a red flag for you to step away from him until you are calm. If your horse is kicking, biting, charging, or rearing, it's time to get professional help.

THE *Myth*

Showing off is always a good plan. Walking under your horse and telling everyone what a terrific person you are and then proving it by doing things that are dangerous is the best way to prove your words. Besides, your horse loves you; he'd never do anything to hurt you.

Happily EVER AFTER

Don't be an idiot. Think about what danger you putting yourself into, and consider the consequences of your actions. Of all the dangerous things to do, walking under a horse to prove how much he trusts you, how well-trained he is and how brave you are may just be the dumbest.

Even the most calm, best trained horse can get startled and his first reaction is to move.

A horse can feel a fly land on him; and his belly is quite sensitive. If your hair or clothing grazes his skin, what do you think he'll do? He will swat at the nuisance—*you*—in the only way he can. If you're lucky, he will simply swish his tail. If not, he will kick at the 'fly'—again, *you*—and will cause you serious harm.

Trust is a good thing, something to be sought after and cherished, but not by walking under your horse. Even the most calm, best trained horse can get startled and his first reaction is to move.

Do not ever purposefully put yourself under a horse. It's just a really bad idea. Walk around your horse, and be sure he knows where you are; do not take a shortcut under his neck or belly. If you're underneath a 1,100 pound animal, it's a good bet you'll be injured or even killed.

THE *Myth*

Groom your horse in his stall, and remember to latch the door so he can't escape. By locking the stall door, you'll be sure to keep your horse in his stall while you groom and saddle him. He can eat his hay while you're getting ready and you won't have to worry about him getting tangled in the lead rope.

Happily EVER AFTER

Locking the door while you are in with him loose is a potentially disastrous decision. If he spooks, he could run over you and if you fall and land underneath him, you could be trampled. It's fine to groom your horse while he is in his stall, if he's wearing a halter while tied. Always keep the door closed, and be ready to get out fast if the need arises. Having him tied means he is secured in one area of a small stall and give you fighting chance of getting out of the way fast enough.

Eleven hundred pounds moving at lightning speed in a twelve-foot-by-twelve-foot stall makes those corners you thought you would duck into seem not quite as convenient as you thought...be sure you can get out fast. Tying your horse while in his stall is a good way to prevent injury to either of you.

Tying your horse while in his stall is a good way to prevent injury to either of you.

★

TIDBIT
Most stalls are twelve feet square, and the average horse is eight feet long; not much room for you to get away if he gets startled and jumps.

THE *Myth*

You've removed his halter and lead and you know he's happy to get to grazing, so you pop him on the rump to send him off fast. It's a game he loves! As he spins to leave, he glances over his shoulder and bucks, but you know he'd never kick you on purpose.

Happily EVER AFTER

You are most vulnerable when releasing your horse into his haven of pasture and freedom. This is particularly true if his equine buddies have already left the gate area and are out of his sight.

Before unbuckling the halter, turn back toward the gate so he faces it. If the other horses are far away, or running wildly hither and yon and your horse is worried, prancing and anxious, it might be best to step out of the gate, close it, and then remove the halter.

Better, if your horse learns that being with you is more fun than being with his equine friends, he won't want to leave. Before taking off his halter, ask him to lower his head, and then scratch his face, behind his ears, or any other 'sweet spot'. Unbuckle the halter and remove it, but keep him with you until you are ready to walk away. Giving a treat is a good way to keep him focused on you too.

Don't turn your back on him until you are far enough away that even if he bolts, you will have time to react. By keeping eye contact, you keep your connection with him open and you encourage him to stay put.

⊍

Before unbuckling the halter, turn back toward the gate so he faces it.

THE *Myth*

Stand facing the horse and hold the halter or bridle using both hands. Be sure your elbows are away from your body and the halter is held at shoulder height or higher. Approach the horse at a brisk walk. When the horse raises his head, yell at him. He will step back, head high, eyes rolling, so take a big hurried stride toward him while yelling for him to lower his head and to stop moving.

Happily EVER AFTER

Rule number one: keep your horse feeling safe at all times, and understand that high hands and loud voices will scare him. Horse's eyes are set to either side of his head so he is better able to see danger from all directions, yet, he can't see directly in front of him. A person approaching a horse straight on may frighten him, so walking at an oblique angle toward his head is a good idea. If the person looks bigger than normal because her hands are up in the air, the horse interprets this as 'pressure' and may become frightened and spook.

The best way to halter a horse is to stand beside him at his shoulder and have him turn his head around toward you. Teach him a head-down cue while he is haltered; either by laying your palm on his "poll," the area just behind his ears or by holding light downward pressure on the lead rope. When he moves his head lower, even by a fraction of an inch, do not follow with your hand, but allow him to escape the pressure. His instant reward is the escape from feeling the touch of your hand

> Horse's eyes are set to either side of his head so he is better able to see danger from all directions, yet, he can't see directly in front of him.

or halter, and he learns to lower his head at your request. Reward him enthusiastically to cement the training.

Teach him to put his nose into the halter, and your life becomes even easier. Using positive reinforcement such as giving treats to teach this helps him to learn quicker and encourages him to try harder. Begin by holding the halter so the nosepiece is open, while offering him the chance to touch it with his nose. When he does, he gets a reward. If you prefer not to offer a treat, a scratch will work just as well. Build upon this action until the horse reaches for the halter or bridle as if to put it on his own.

When approaching, be sure your horse can see you, and do not approach him in a hurried manner. Keep your hands low and your voice soft. Be aware of his blind spots and let him know where you are at all times so he is not spooked. Teaching your horse to lower his head and put his nose into the halter makes catching him fun and easy!

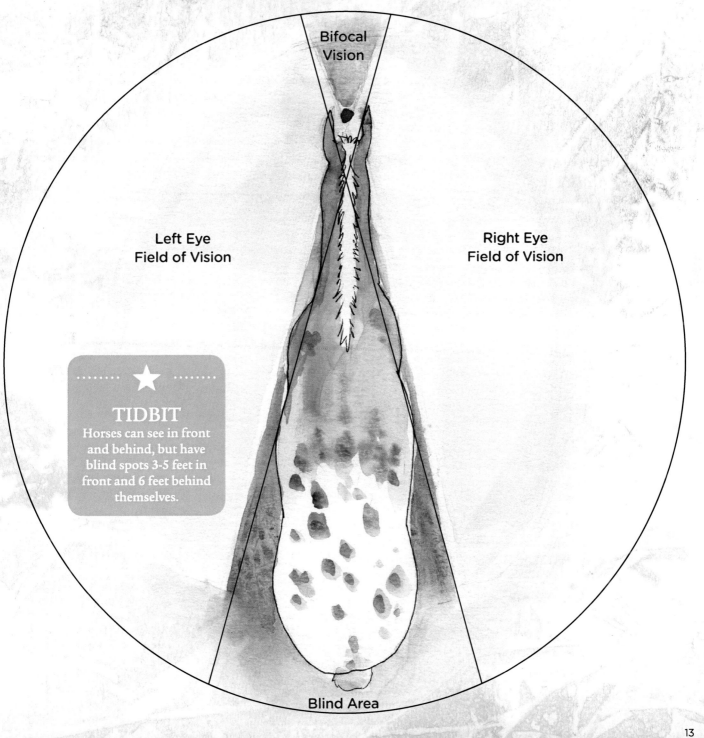

Bifocal
Vision

Left Eye
Field of Vision

Right Eye
Field of Vision

★

TIDBIT

Horses can see in front
and behind, but have
blind spots 3-5 feet in
front and 6 feet behind
themselves.

Blind Area

THE *Myth*

Buy a horse based on his looks, his color, and how he looks at you; particularly if it's your first horse. Look only at horses with spots or maybe a buckskin or palomino. Choose based on looks alone, and buy from a photo, online, sight unseen if you like the photo of his face, (those eyes!), and his color.

If you go to look at a horse in person and he leans his chin or forehead on your shoulder, it's sign that he is your horse. If he's pretty, and carries his head high and prances with his tail floating behind him, grab him up quick, before someone else comes along and grabs him. No time for vet checks and trainer approval—move!

Happily EVER AFTER

Beginners and first time buyers let their hearts and emotions determine which horse is best for them, but the prettiest, sweetest horse may not be the best choice.

Many old cowboy sayings come to mind: You can't ride "pretty". You can't ride spots. Pretty is as pretty does. You can't ride color. However, pretty horses do make nice lawn ornaments.

> Training,
> temperament, breed,
> and conformation of
> the animal must be
> verified and evaluated.

All sarcasm aside, buying a horse is nothing like buying a car or a new dryer. It's easy to quantitatively measure and compare machines; you can even go to *Consumer Reports* and see what others think of a particular brand. Once you've researched the item, choosing the best looking car is fun and not life threatening. Not the case in horse shopping; especially if buying for a child or if it's your first horse. What you see and are most drawn to is the 'chrome', the polish and the cute face.

What's most important is the soundness, the suitability and the overall matching of your personality with his. Training, temperament, breed, and conformation of the animal must be verified and evaluated.

Working with a knowledgeable, qualified trainer is essential and you must be prepared to take her advice. A sweet, pretty horse may have hidden issues under the hood and the last popular saying to remember is that "no good horse ever comes in a bad color".

THE *Myth*

No reason to pay for a horse, look, people dump horses by turning them loose every day. Free horses are a great deal, take two! And you don't need registration papers, what difference does it make?

 *Happily* EVER AFTER

★

TIDBIT
There is no such thing as a free horse.

Good horses are the result of good breeding, good training and good care. These things do not come cheap, so why would the perfect horse be free?

The purchase price of a horse is likely the least of your expenses as you enter the horse world. The saying "you get what you pay for" is not always true, but have as healthy a budget as you are able to afford, and plan to spend some money, especially if buying a horse for a child. Get the horse you can ride today, not after he goes through training, or grows up or gets over whatever ails him in the moment.

"Free horse" translates to one needing time to grow up, training, medical care, special feed, expensive supplements, corrective shoes, rehabilitative work, or any number of equally expensive things. He also may be very old, or may have chronic problems that only worsen with time such as arthritis, navicular disease, or ringbone. When considering a 'free' horse, beware, and enlist the help of a veterinarian and trainer before taking that particular horse home. Some ailments are worth working through, but without a veterinarian's advice, you won't know how to tell.

You will likely pay a trainer more to bring a young, green, un-broke horse along than you will if you buy one that is ready to ride now. Be sure and get expert help and a pre-purchase exam complete with radiographs (x-rays) if anything seems off.

Spend a little more up-front on hiring someone to help you choose the right horse and a veterinarian to do a pre-purchase exam.

♘

The purchase price of a horse is likely the least of your expenses as you enter the horse world.

Do Not Hire A Trainer Before Purchasing Your First Horse.

THE *Myth*

You rode as a child at summer camp, you took lessons when you were ten years-old, you ride trail horses on every vacation, and the guides even let you run! You can stay on and you know what you want to own. Clearly, you know all you need to know to buy a horse.

★

TIDBIT
Buying the wrong horse can harm more than just your ego.

Happily EVER AFTER

An inexperienced buyer won't know if the horse is lame or be able to see any number of problems that a professional can. The worst case scenario includes serious injury or even death to a buyer. In some states, the law sides with the seller since you are knowingly taking a chance around horses. If you are injured, the problem then becomes financial as well as physical.

A beginner simply doesn't have the expertise to 'read' the body language of the animal and will instead believe what the seller tells them. An experienced and qualified trainer can tell more in a ten minute conversation with a seller or by looking at photos or videos of your prospect than you are likely to know after a three hour in-person meeting. Here's why: Trainers work with hundreds of animals and people. Their experience gives them the ability to see things you won't know to look for, such as lameness issues, other physical issues, emotional problems, and holes in the horse's training.

A good trainer has an experienced eye for things sellers do to make a horse look 'better' than he is. Things like shoes that mask a lameness, or tacking up before you arrive in order to hide behavioral issues, or riding the horse down

The worst case scenario includes serious injury or even death to a buyer.

so he's tired, Some unethical sellers even drug horses so they will appear calm and quiet. Not all sellers are bad, but enough are to warrant getting help to stack the deck in your favor. Buying a horse 'blindly' is like playing Russian roulette with a loaded gun. You may get lucky or you may decide to get on a horse that is dangerous, unsound, or unsuitable.

Finding the right horse is different from buying a car or a bicycle. Finding the right horse with the right personality, ability and training level to ensure a life-long relationship. A trainer can see if the match is good or not and this will save you, the buyer a lot of headache, heartache and money in the long run. A good trainer can also advise you to walk away before you spend money on a pre-purchase, too; if there is an obvious physical issue.

All sellers are not honest and will not watch out for your best interest. Spending money by getting professional help is beneficial because you won't have to buy and sell horse after horse searching by trial and error. Matching horse to rider is essential and a qualified trainer saves you time and money in the long run.

You Don't Need A Veterinarian To Look Over The Horse You Want To Purchase.

THE *Myth*

Do not get a pre-purchase exam on a horse you want to buy. Why bother? You can tell he's just fine! He walks and trots and he's so pretty! Besides, if something was wrong, the owner would tell you.

Happily EVER AFTER

Sellers want to sell the horse and make some money or they may just want to get rid of a headache-causing pain in the rear animal. Some problems are physical and others are emotional, and either way, many sellers deliberately hide a known problem by using drugs on the horse to mask pain or temperament. Sometimes, a horse is too hot (high strung) for a beginner, but to sell him to someone unsuspecting, the seller will drug the horse to hide his true problems.

Some tell-tale signs of drugging or overwork include the animal being tacked up and ridden when you arrive, sweat marks clearly visible, dull eyes, listless tail, stumbling, lethargic, low-head and uninterested in surroundings, slack lower lip, or recent bathing, thus hiding sweat marks.

A first-time buyer or a beginner is usually not qualified to evaluate the soundness of a horse.

As far as soundness goes, no one has x-ray vision, but professionals can tell by watching, if a horse moves in a way that indicates a problem. A first-time buyer or a beginner is usually not qualified to evaluate the soundness of a horse. The saying, "No feet, no horse" means just that...if the horse has something wrong with him such as navicular or coffin bone degeneration/rotation, you won't know without radiographs (x-rays).

If you buy a horse without a pre-purchase exam performed by a licensed veterinarian, you simply won't know what you are buying and may discover you have a lame, unrideable horse that you must care for just to be able to sell him yourself.

Get a licensed veterinarian to health check your potential purchase, including x-rays, before you buy him.

DEATH TIP

13

Getting A Package Deal Of Two-For-One Is The Best Way To Buy A Horse.

THE *Myth*

Buy a pregnant mare as your first horse-and you get two for the price of one. It's a screamin' hot deal and you can raise the baby yourself.

TIDBIT
A horse isn't mature until age seven or eight; see Dr. Deb Bennett's research on rate of growth for all breeds. www.womenandhorses.com/newsletter-2006january.html

Happily EVER AFTER

There is a long list of reasons for not doing this, including, but not limited to expertise, expense, and the amount of time required to raise a foal.

While pregnant, the mare has an essential need for exercise, but you have to know how much is too much. From the eight month of pregnancy until foaling in her eleventh month, she will be out of commission for anything other than light riding (no jumping, no gymkhanas, no hard mountainous rides, no cutting or sorting), and remains so until the foal is able to tag along, but even then, the foal can't do long, hard rides. The foal can be weaned when he is about six-months-old, so about a year will pass before your mare can be ridden as usual.

If there are problems at time of parturition (foaling), or if the foal has health issues, you are responsible for saving his life. This can be expensive beyond your wildest imaginings.

Buy a horse your trainer and veterinarian approve so you can ride immediately and enjoy a long lifetime of happiness with him.

Raising a foal is expensive; and he won't be a riding horse for at least three years, maybe longer as he is not mature enough until that age to start under saddle.

Training takes both time and money, and since the mare will need refreshers after having almost a year off, there will that added expense. If this is your first horse, you are not equipped to train a youngster alone.

If trained incorrectly, the horse will require re-training which takes much longer than if the job is done right the first time.

Babies are cute, but not the best fit for the beginner or first time horse owner. Buy a horse your trainer and veterinarian approve so you can ride immediately and enjoy a long lifetime of happiness with him. There is no such thing as a free horse; even a foal that is still in-utero when you buy his dam.

THE *Myth*

Stallions are prettier. They prance and arch their necks and you can breed him and make money, too!

> ⋯⋯⋯ ★ ⋯⋯⋯
> ### TIDBIT
> Surgery is the only way to remedy for cryptorchidism—the retention of one or both testicles. Without surgery, he may look like a gelding, but act like a stallion.

 EVER AFTER ⋯⋯⋯⋯⋯⋯⋯⋯⋯⋯⋯⋯⋯

No beginner, novice, intermediate, or first-time horse buyer should ever consider buying a stallion. Even the most experienced horse person should think twice before adding a stallion to the barn.

Stallions are not bad horses, but besides eating, they are interested in one thing only, and that is breeding. Holding their attention can be a challenge to say the least—yes, even if they are trained and older and 'don't act like a stud'. If you don't know how to handle a stallion, you will likely find yourself in the hospital, in the courtroom, or both.

Breeding a stallion for some extra cash is not a responsible choice for the novice horse owner.

Housing a stallion is another point to consider. Many people feel he should not be kept with other horses and risk injury to himself or the other animals he is kept with, but this is not a good life for him; he is more than just a breeding machine. However, mares become a 'resource' and it is the claiming and guarding of resources that leads to aggression in horses. If he decides that you are a threat to his resources, he may challenge you and at 1,100 pounds (a smaller stallion), he

will likely win. He may decide your family, friends and pets are a threat. Again, he wins. Stallions are known to go through, over or under any obstacle to get to what they want—mares—so fencing must be secure.

Breeding a stallion for some extra cash is not a responsible choice for the novice horse owner. Too many 'backyard' breeders have no idea what traits constitute a quality breeding animal, so the resulting offspring have a good chance of ending up as part of the food chain in the horse slaughter industry.

Non-qualified owners who choose to pasture breed their stallion to local mares are taking a huge health risk to both their horse and the mare in with him. Injury, infection and transmitting of sexual diseases are likely in the pasture breeding scenario.

Stallions are not a good choice for anyone other than an equine professional, and make wonderful geldings within six months after castration.

DEATH TIP

15

*Get A Young Horse
So You Can Learn Together.*

THE *Myth*

Buy the prettiest, youngest foal and raise it, especially if it's your first horse, or if buying for your child. You can learn together, you'll bond better and if buying for your child, she and the foal will most certainly become best friends.

Remember to choose based on color and markings, and how 'sweet' the horse acts toward people, and if you aren't completely sure, ask your neighbor's opinion.

Happily EVER AFTER

There is an old saying, "Green on green results in black and blue," and it means that a green (unfinished, usually young) horse is not a good match for any beginner or most children (greenhorns) and can lead to unscheduled dismounts and consequent bruising.

Buying an older horse that is forgiving of a human's mistakes is a much better choice for the beginner or child. Having an older horse doesn't mean he'll take care of you or your child, but he's less likely to blow up (act like a wild horse) for minor indiscretions on the rider's part.

Once fear becomes part of a beginner's horse experience, the dream is shattered. An inexperienced person simply doesn't know enough to keep the horse feeling safe, which results in a fearful horse ridden by a now terrified rider.

Once fear becomes part of a beginner's horse experience, the dream is shattered.

The result can be truly devastating on all levels, with the horse being blamed and labeled as a renegade when in reality he was reacting to stimuli in a 'good horse' manner.

Oftentimes, the result is that the horse is sold repeatedly as his fear increases and his trust of the world diminishes and makes no sense to him. Finally, he either lands with a good trainer or truly does become what people say he is—a rank horse because he's just trying to keep himself safe. These horses face a dim outlook and some end up going to slaughter and dying through no fault of their own.

Beginners, first-time horse owners, buy the horse you can ride today and work with a qualified and experienced riding instructor. Beginners can avoid injury and pain by choosing a forgiving, confidence-building horse.

23

DEATH TIP

16

When Selling, Omit, Lie, And Deny.

THE *Myth*

Tell potential buyers as little as possible and exaggerate the things you think they want to hear. You have a spotted horse, call him a Paint. You have a horse that bucks; omit that fact. Your horse is prone to colic; don't say anything. Your horse has a recent diagnosis of navicular disease? Hush!

Happily EVER AFTER

On average, horses change hands in the United States about every two years, so selling ethically can help secure them a life-long home.

Avoiding the facts regarding the sale of an unruly or unsound horse puts the buyer at risk and makes you culpable for negligence. Knowledge of a preexisting condition such as a physical or behavioral problem means you should divulge the truth. Truth in sales is essential and you'd want a seller to tell you everything they could before you or your child got injured.

It is dangerous to all involved, including the horse, to lie about any problems you've had with a horse. Tell all; the buyer knows what she can handle. The added benefit is that you'll have a good reputation as an honest seller if you ever sell other horses.

On average, horses change hands in the United States about every two years, so selling ethically can help secure them a life-long home.

TIDBIT
A Paint is a horse registered with the American Paint Horse Association and will only have Paints, Quarter horses and Thoroughbreds in their pedigrees.

THE *Myth*

You have a mare you can't get along with, especially when she's in heat. She is cranky most days; pushy and nasty on the ground, and when you ride with others, all she does is pee, squeal and kick. It seems she is constantly in heat, and your neighbor says if you breed her, her mood will change.

You've reached the end of your rope and decide it's time to move her along. Thing is, no one wants to buy a cranky, crazy horse. It makes sense that since she is somewhat reasonable when not in heat, breeding her will help make a quick sale.

Happily EVER AFTER

This is not a good solution for a mare who acts up while in heat because even if it did help (which it won't), the behavior returns within week of giving birth, during her first heat cycle. Best to hire a trainer to help you with her behavior and to decide if her acting out is due to lack of training or if it really is due to her heat cycles and hormones.

Your trainer will need to assess the horse's training level, and then will likely recommend a veterinarian examine your mare to rule out any physical issues. A veterinarian

A veterinarian can examine the mare and determine if hormonal or ovary problems are responsible for her undesirable attitude.

can examine the mare and determine if hormonal or ovary problems such as cysts or tumors are responsible for the horse's undesirable attitude.

If her reproductive system is healthy, the vet can suggest other options such as temporary hormone therapy to help curb the unwanted behavior. Oftentimes, the 'fix' is a matter of her getting a shot to help her feel better.

Breeding a horse you don't like or want is irresponsible and may result in a foal with similar unwanted behavior.

★ TIDBIT
A mare with reproductive-system issues may act like a stallion, buck, become aggressive, or even appear lame.

THE *Myth*

You bought good hay, grain, and supplements. Just feed him twice a day and all is well concerning your horse's diet.

Happily EVER AFTER

Just like us, horses have nutritional requirements that must be met, and learning what and how much he needs is important. Beyond that, you must know if the roughage you are feeding (hay) is good quality and what minerals and vitamins it may be lacking.

Be certain to examine all hay, grain and any supplements at each feeding. Look for any sign of contamination, discoloration or anything that looks out of the ordinary.

Learn to tell if your hay has gone bad by knowing what moldy hay looks, smells and feels like, in contrast to clean fresh hay. Moldy hay will be heavier than normal, darker in color and oftentimes, a white or gray powder will waft up from it when you move or toss it. There may or may not be a distinct moldy smell. Do not feed hay that is remotely suspicious. Better to toss a few dollars' worth of hay than to cause your horse to be sick. Besides, you'll save yourself hundreds in vet bills.

Mouse droppings in grain can cause salmonella poisoning in a horse, and can spread from horse to horse, so if you see any, toss the entire lot. Same for supplements; if you think they've gone bad do not feed to your horse.

Check your horse's feed for mold, foreign objects, mice or opossum droppings.

Be certain to examine all hay, grain and any supplements at each feeding.

TIDBIT
When in doubt,
throw it out.

THE *Myth*

Feeding a horse on the ground is bad because he'll eat dirt and get sand colic. Better to get him one of the tall metal feeders so he won't put his head down to eat dirt.

TIDBIT
Feeding from high off the ground can cause back muscles to atrophy over time, while neck muscles and nerves may become pinched and impaired.

Happily EVER AFTER

Horses have long necks and long noses, with eyes set to the sides of their heads so they can graze. They are foragers and in general, and are built to eat their feed at ground level.

Horses need their heads to be low while eating so that he inhales fewer hay particles and other irritants. A lower head also helps his airways drain and allows him to flush out any inhaled dust or hay particles.

While feeding on the ground is not desirable—as the horse may ingest waste, parasite eggs, sand, or gravel—it is a good idea to feed as near the ground as possible. An old water trough with holes poked into the bottom for drainage make the most ideal feeders, but anything similar works well.

Feeding horses with hay net 'pillows' are a good idea, too. Just be sure your horse can't get tangled in them, especially if he's shod—you may need to put the pillow into an old water trough or build a box to secure it. These pillows work as 'slow feeders' as they have small, elasticized netting the horse must pull hay through in order to eat. Hay nets can be hung at chest height and are a slow-feed method that keeps the hay off the ground and the horses happy.

Another great solution is feeding on rubber mats. This works well as long as you sweep debris from the mat before each meal.

Horses need their heads to be low while eating so that he inhales fewer hay particles and other irritants.

DEATH TIP

20

▾

Boarding? Don't Worry About A Thing.

THE *Myth*

Owning a horse is easy when you don't have to concern yourself with what your horse eats, what his living conditions are, who he is stabled next to. After all, he's boarded—that's what you pay for and they should take care of everything!

Happily EVER AFTER

⭐
TIDBIT
Educate yourself on what constitutes good hay, good fencing, and proper horse care before choosing a place to keep your horse.

Your horse's well-being, safety, and health are your responsibility, no matter where he lives or who is caring for him. This includes his physical, emotional, and mental health. His overall happiness is just as important as what he eats.

Prioritize yours and your horse's needs when choosing a boarding facility. It's good to consider the following:

- Location
- Cleanliness
- Overall condition of the place
- Feed quality and frequency
- Fencing type
- Turnout
- Safety of the barn and fences
- The caregivers' level of experience

Prioritize yours and your horse's needs when choosing a boarding facility.

Talking with other boarders is a great way to find out about a place that might best suit you and your horse. Internet searches, talking with your vet, farrier, and trainer may put you in contact with the right facility. Some questions to ask include:

- Do the caretakers live on site?
- Do they do night checks?
- Are they good about communicating with the boarders?
- Is there a resident trainer, or are you allowed to bring in your own?

You and your horse will be happier if you do your homework and research before moving him into substandard living quarters.

DEATH
TIP
21

No Need For A Tetanus
Vaccination For Your Horse
—Or Yourself.

THE *Myth*

There is no reason to vaccinate against tetanus; you're healthy and fine and so is your horse.

TETANUS TOXOID VACCINATION SCHEDULE FOR HORSES:

- **Vaccination may begin at 3 months of age.**

- **Initially 2 injections should be given 4-6 weeks apart**

- **The first tetanus booster should be given a year later**

- **Boosters are required every 2 to 5 years per your veterinarian**

Happily EVER AFTER

Tetanus is a serious disease of the nervous system caused by bacterial poison that's produced by Clostridium tetani bacteria. It lives and thrives in horse manure and enters the body—yours or your horse's—through a cut or abrasion.

Preventive measures taken may keep your horse from becoming seriously ill if he is exposed to the bacteria. It is simple; just vaccinate against tetanus as advised by your veterinarian. If an unvaccinated horse is injured, tetanus antitoxin should be given to provide immediate protection. There are two kinds of tetanus vaccines, tetanus antitoxin, which is short term (3 weeks) protection and tetanus toxoid is longer term (1-5 years) protection depending on the brand. Both may be given on the same day, but be sure and inject at different sites.

Humans also need tetanus vaccinations and must wear proper shoes and gloves to help limit exposure to the tetanus bacteria. Just like the horse, people will need tetanus antitoxin if not up to date on tetanus vaccination. Be sure and get your own tetanus vaccine once every ten years.

Clean your and your horse's wounds immediately with warm water and soap. Never use hydrogen peroxide on your horse; it dries out and damages the tissue.

Tetanus toxin attacks nerves controlling the muscles of the body and causes muscular stiffness and spasm that make it hard for him to move. The third eyelid may protrude over his eye. He may hold his tail straight out behind him. Everyday things, like a loud sound, bright light or even your touch may make him look worse. In advanced cases the horse will sweat, worry, spasm, convulse and die from respiratory failure.

Tetanus toxin attacks nerves controlling the muscles of the body and causes muscular stiffness and spasm that make it hard for him to move.

TIDBIT

If your horse stands with his front legs
stretched out in front of him and his head low,
obviously, something is wrong, but it doesn't
necessarily indicate tetanus. Call your vet!

DEATH TIP
22

Love Bites Don't
Mean He's Naughty.

THE *Myth*

It's cute when he nibbles at your clothing and tugs at your pocket. Your horse likes to nuzzle your pocket looking for hidden treats and when he doesn't find them, he nips at your jacket and gives a tug. He's such a nut! Besides you don't mind when he inadvertently bites you, instead of fabric; you know he didn't mean anything.

Happily EVER AFTER

The biggest issue with allowing this behavior is that you are teaching him that his grabbing you with his teeth is acceptable. Horses are huge animals with large teeth and a lot of jaw power. Even if you don't think there is anything wrong with his nipping you, there is the possibility of him biting others. What if a small child is near and your big, goofy, cuter than all other horses bites her? Many outcomes are possible and not a single one is acceptable.

Setting boundaries that you are happy with is what counts, and if you are okay with having a horse that bites, then sure, allow him to put his mouth on people. However, even keeping a lawyer on retainer and carrying a healthy insurance policy, you are likely to lose the resulting lawsuit. Never allow a horse to put his mouth on you or your clothing.

★
TIDBIT
Horses bite down with 800 pounds per square inch. In comparison, a lion's bite force is 650 psi.

Never allow a horse to put his mouth on you or your clothing.

THE *Myth*

You finally got a horse and want to train him just like you did your dog. You know you'll get the same enthusiastic, tail-wagging, tongue-lolling results. After all, he is just a big puppy and should be dog-like in his willingness and desire to please you.

When you arrive at the barn and he acts up—bouncing off the walls, tossing his head, not wanting to let you catch him, laugh and tell everyone how much like a Golden Retriever he is. Remind them and yourself that he wants every minute of his day to be spent in your company. Since you haven't been able to get out until now, he's upset and he is punishing you.

Happily EVER AFTER

Equines are not canines. Very little about the two species is similar. One is a prey animal and the other is not, and this difference alone is enough to warrant evaluating how to handle them. Your dog lives to please you and be with you. He yearns for your company, watches for your car to pull into the driveway and follows you happily.

Horses are not driven by the desire to be constantly with you or to gain your approval. They like to be with you, but as hard as this is to hear—they like *not* being with you, too.

Your expectation that your horse respond as a dog can confuse him. For example, your desire for them to 'be sweet' or to 'hug' you, might, instead, cause them to do some undesirable behaviors, like leaning on you, encroaching on your space, or even biting.

A horse is not a 1,100 pound Pomeranian and should never be treated as such.

> ★
> ### TIDBIT
> Horses like to please, but they don't live to please humans.

> Horses are not driven by the desire to be constantly with you or to gain your approval.

THE *Myth*

It's a warm summer day and you're strolling along with your horse and laughing with your friends, enjoying the scenery and happily chatting. Out of nowhere, your arm is yanked from its socket and you're pitched forward so fast, you think you're going to fall down on the ground. Your horse is oblivious to your discomfort as he stops midstride to eat some lush greenery growing alongside the path.

Happily EVER AFTER

Although it's fun to talk with friends while spending time with your horse, remember to keep yourself in the present moment and aware of your surroundings and what your horse is thinking. You will be better able to guide him with expertise and confidence, and avoid any surprises.

Horses never stop communicating their wants or needs; all you need to do is learn to recognize what his body language means. Most horses look with their eye first, then their ear will tip toward that yummy morsel, and then, the nostril and mouth follow. If you stop the action at the eye-looking stage, you won't have to have an argument over his eating or doing the job at hand. However, if you allow him to get to the third step because you haven't stopped him, he will absolutely surprise you and gain his reward of eating fresh, green grass.

By allowing him to grab food while on a walk or a trail ride, you reinforce behavior that you don't want. You have inadvertently trained him to eat whenever he chooses, even if you don't want him to. In the equine world, if you are not leading, you must have given your horse that role. Let your horse call the shots and you might not like his choices.

> By allowing him to grab food while on a walk or a trail ride, you reinforce behavior that you don't want.

TIDBIT
Horses, by nature, like to either lead or follow, so if you don't want to be his leader, he will assume that role.

THE *Myth*

You're only going to the barn for a minute, so wearing flip-flops are fine. You think it's okay to go to the barn or pasture or corral wearing sandals. Cleaning the stalls in any kind of footwear is good, too. No worries!

Happily EVER AFTER

TIDBIT

Wearing boots that are meant for the barn exclusively will keep your other footwear from smelling of the barn, too!

The average horse weighs about 1,100 pounds which is over half a ton. If he steps on your foot—whether you are wearing boots or not—it hurts! If he steps down, and then spins while on top of you, it really hurts and you will likely have bruised, fractured, or broken bones. If you are not wearing leather boots, the tender skin on the top of your foot will be shaved off by the horse's hoof, leaving you with broken bones and cut skin.

Leather boots won't keep your bones from breaking, but they do give you more protection than any other shoe you may choose.

Boots are essential if you are anywhere near a horse—for both riding and groundwork. Horses are big and they move fast, and though you may think you can avoid being stepped on, you're wrong. Dress properly and wear protective clothing, including the right boots when with your horse.

Dress properly and wear protective clothing, including the right boots when with your horse.

THE *Myth*

If your horse doesn't 'get it'—he doesn't stop when you pull back, he won't collect, or won't go fast enough—you just need a bigger, better, badder tool to help him see things your way.

For riding difficulties, a different bit is usually the first change you will want to make, since he's obviously become desensitized to his old one and no longer obeys the cues.

Happily EVER AFTER

In general, artificial aids allow you to significantly increase the pressure you put on your horse. Since most people think more pressure is the answer to any problem they encounter; either under saddle or in hand, the first change made will be to choose a new, bigger, better gadget that will help the horse see the error of his ways and become the perfect horse. The trouble with this line of thinking is that by intensifying the pressure, the problem will either worsen or a whole new set will appear.

Before increasing pressure to get different results, be sure your horse is safe, comfortable, and physically and emotionally able to do what you want. Ask a trainer for help and advice and pay her for her time. If she wants to use a bigger hammer, find a better trainer.

Most of the time, a horse refuses to do what you want due to pain, fear or the desire to be somewhere else. When your horse doesn't comply, ask yourself what you're doing wrong before punishing him.

Most of the time, a horse refuses to do what you want due to pain, fear or the desire to be somewhere else.

★

TIDBIT
Change his mind and you'll change his feet.

A good checklist to ask when you encounter problems with your horse is:

1. Does he feel safe?
2. Is he physically comfortable? This includes back, teeth, and leg, hoof, and neck issues.
3. Does his tack fit properly? Is it in good repair? Is the saddle pad clean and free of debris?
4. Are you in the correct frame of mind? Are you happy, present, and calm?
5. Is your body position and body language correct and consistent? Are you sitting centered and balanced?
6. Does he truly and completely understand what you are asking? Are you expecting too much from him?
7. Is he able to do what you want? A 13 hand pony will have a hard time jumping a six foot fence, be sure you aren't expecting too much.

THE *Myth*

Teach your horse to chase you when he's loose. It's a fun game and you can show people how he acts like a dog. Besides, your horse loves this game.

Happily EVER AFTER

In the language of the horse, the one chasing another is establishing himself as dominant; usually because he is guarding some resource. Teaching a horse to run after you may result in him thinking he is dominant. By making you run, he may consider you to be subservient to him. In some instances, horses are labeled "mean" because they become over exuberant when people enter their paddock and they crowd, thinking the fun and games are happening.

Horses run faster than humans and can hold the pace much longer. If you trip and fall, are you certain he will be able to stop before running over you?

When horses chase something—a dog, a coyote, a human—they may bite it or stomp it once close enough. If your horse bit you or gets you down and stomped you, the results would be disastrous. Don't encourage this behavior. Never allow a horse to chase you.

When horses chase something—a dog, a coyote, a human—they may bite it or stomp it once close enough.

DEATH TIP
28

Prancing Is Pretty.

THE *Myth*

Your horse is prettiest when his head is up, his nostrils are flaring, and he's dancing. Whether in hand or under saddle, everyone likes a high-headed horse, right? Prancing, snorting, and rearing is even better; just look at how his mane and tail fly!

Happily EVER AFTER

Horses convey what they are thinking and feeling by using almost every part of their bodies. As prey animals, it is not in their best interest to shout to one another, "Hey, a lion is on the hill over there!" and so they have evolved to communicate through body language, not words. High headed horses may look prettier, but an experienced horse person will immediately look for what the underlying problem might be. Fear, pain and excitement all cause a horse to carry his head high. Determining the reason for him being high-headed is important so that you may help him be more comfortable.

Fear, pain and excitement all cause a horse to carry his head high.

Experienced horse people know that a high head is a sign from the horse that he feels unsafe and is silently warning other horses to be aware of the danger he perceives. When a horse exhibits this fearful stance, he will appear rock solid and statuesque. His ears point straight toward whatever he is worried about and his breathing changes from longer slower breaths to fast and shallow as he tries to use all of his senses to find what the source of his worry is.

Because a high-headed horse can see further and smell scents in the air easier, a high head carriage indicates that the horse feels threatened, there is some sort of problem, or he is so excited, he can't think straight. A grazing horse is more vulnerable, so for him to lower his head, or graze, he must feel calm and safe. When agitated and fretting, horses will often stand stock-still before exploding into frenzied and fast motion.

Although not 100 percent effective, teaching a horse a 'head down cue' is a good idea, as it helps him focus his attention and give you the reins, so to speak. To train, simply give a cue like your hand resting lightly on his neck if you are riding—just in front of the withers; or a use a light downward pressure on the lead, if you are walking next to him. When he lowers his head, even a millimeter, praise and reward him. Repeat 101 times until he responds consistently.

A horse with a flying mane and tail is on high-alert and pretty as this may be, it is a visual signal that you should beware. His instinct is to react first and think later. Be sure you are attentive and able to handle such an emotional state as your horse may appear to ignore any cues you give him—at least until he feels safe enough to come back to you mentally and then physically.

THE *Myth*

Anchor the rope to the inside of the trailer and it will surely make him step up and in, because he'll realize he can't get away. If you can winch him an inch at a time, he'll eventually see the brilliance in your plan, give up, and you will be on your way.

Happily EVER AFTER

Tying a horse's head to the front of the trailer can result in injury or death should he pull back and hang himself or rear and crack his head open.

The most effective way of training a horse to like anything you want him to do—in this case a trailer—is to associate the new or frightening object with something good and desired, like food or comfort. A scared animal will react differently than a calm horse. And a horse seeing a trailer for the first time may not react at all since he has no negative connotations associated with it.

Begin training your horse to load by teaching him a few simple commands such as lowering his head, moving away from pressure, stepping up onto a platform, walking through narrow openings and backing down a step. You should be able to move your horse in any direction; forward, backward, sideways and he should move just his front end or back end when you ask.

★

TIDBIT
Force should never be a part of your handling any horse.

Once he is comfortable with the cues you've taught him, you are ready to move on to loading him.

By teaching him that you are calm and not in a hurry, he will trust you and will learn to load on command. If the horse raises his head and sets his feet, go back to a lesson he understands completely, before asking him to do anything new. Once he is comfortable with the cues you've taught him, you are ready to move on to loading him.

As soon as your horse sees the trailer as a happy place, the amount of stress involved in going anywhere diminishes. Teach him a specific signal to load, then practice often, even if you don't go anywhere.

DEATH TIP

30

▼

Reel Him In Like A Big Fish
And He'll Load Every Time.

THE *Myth*

To load a horse into a trailer, pull that rope taut and don't give him any slack. You walk to the trailer, hoping your horse will get in with no fuss. He doesn't. You pull harder. He pulls back. You feel your anger rise and try to subdue it, but it's time to go. You dig your heels in and pull even harder; he rears and cuts his head on the trailer top.

Happily EVER AFTER

Same two rules apply here—horses move away from negative pressure, not toward it and he must, at all times, feel safe.

Since predators live in small, dark places, it only makes sense your horse doesn't want to get in the trailer. Although your horse doesn't deal with cougars on a daily basis, he is hardwired genetically to know that caves should be avoided. (This is also why many horses stand in the rain instead of in their stalls if given the choice.) By asking your horse to get into a trailer, you are asking him to forget about what he instinctively knows is true. The horse sees a confined dark space when he looks into a trailer. He doesn't understand that it's a fun, easy way to travel.

Every foal's mother teaches him to move away from pressure. Watch a mare reprimand or push her foal away—she never ever pulls on his head. Pulling on the head is not a good cue, pushing from behind is what he'll respond to best. Instead of responding to constant pulling on his head by moving forward, a horse will sit back on his haunches, dig his feet in, and refuse to go anywhere.

The more you pull, the more frightened he becomes and eventually, when he can't get away from you by moving sideways or backwards, he will avoid coming toward the pressure by choosing the only option left; up. This usually ends with a vet bill for the stitches it takes to sew up his cracked open head.

Remember, he wants to feel safe at all times, and a non-cave dwelling animal won't see a cavernous metal box as being a safe place to willingly walk into.

> ♄
>
> **Watch a mare reprimand or push her foal away— she never ever pulls on his head.**

TIDBIT
Pulling on a horse's head
when he wants to back will start a fight,
and face it; you'll never win in a tug
of war with a half-ton animal.

DEATH TIP

31

He's In The Trailer,
Slam The Door!

THE *Myth*

Your horse finally gets in the trailer. Slam that door before he backs out so fast, you can't stop him. Hope that your helpful assistant won't get flattened in the process.

Happily EVER AFTER

TIDBIT

If you have a horse that blasts out at unloading time, try parking your trailer over a puddle. It won't hurt him, but it can teach him to look where he is going and unload carefully!

> If you slam the door, you confirm that his fears are justified and that you are not to be trusted.

If you slam the door, you confirm that his fears are justified and that you are not to be trusted. This is the opposite of your long-term goal and if he could talk, he'd say, "I knew it!"

The best way to train him to load is to go slowly and allow him to step out when he needs to, and don't pull on the lead. Think of your horse as if he were a large house cat. Cats hate confinement just as horses do, if they 'think' they can escape, but choose to stay put, they eventually learn to trust being confined.

Practice loading, standing, and backing on command until you know your horse understands he is to stand quietly. Now, you can begin swinging the door closed, but only an inch or two, until you can open, shut and tap on it without the horse moving a muscle. Only then should you shut the door.

Horses need time and reassurance when learning new things; remember "the wait" and be patient!

DEATH TIP

32

▼

Use The Escape Hatch.

THE *Myth*

When you walk into a two-horse trailer with your horse in tow, there is a small escape door for you to get out as he gets in. Be sure the escape hatch is open and ready for you to get out of the trailer.

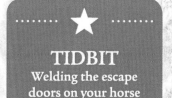

★

TIDBIT
Welding the escape doors on your horse trailer may save a life.

Happily EVER AFTER

Most straight-load trailers come equipped with 'suicide doors' which are labeled as 'escape doors'. These are small openings that you must crouch through to get out of the trailer. The theory is that you load your horse by walking in ahead of him and then crawl out the hatch before he is on top of you. Even if you are super-fast and can bend over, duck your head, lift first one, then the other leg and climb out quickly, your horse may decide that since you led him in, he is supposed to follow you out through the small door. Best case, your horse doesn't load because you're in his way. Worst case, you get smashed, trampled, or killed because you couldn't get out fast enough.

If you happen to get out in time to avoid getting crushed, you may find your horse has indeed followed you and is still following. He can get his head, neck, and one or two front legs through that same door, but then he will be stuck and unable to get back in or out. This scenario results in serious injury or death to the animal and usually, a blowtorch to dismantle your trailer.

Do not ever use the escape door and instead, teach your horse to load while you stand outside, or pull a long rope out the hay window to guide him into the trailer.

If you happen to get out in time to avoid getting crushed, you may find your horse has indeed followed you and is still following.

DEATH TIP
33

Make The First Few Trailer Rides Short

THE *Myth*

While training to load and haul, don't drive far; keep those first rides to under twenty minutes so he gets used to the trailer.

Happily EVER AFTER

When stressed, adrenaline surges through the horse's body, and he needs time to let the adrenaline subside before stopping and short rides aren't long enough. If you can have a buddy horse ride along with him on his first outing, go for a ride lasting more than one and a half hours. Stop periodically to check on him offer praise, treats, and water. This process will generally help your horse become a happy and confident trailer rider.

Stop periodically to check on him offer praise, treats, and water.

A horse that has been hauled four to twelve times usually will get right in and stand while you close the door. However, once he learns that a trailer ride is rough, bouncy, loud, lonely, and scary; he may backslide in his progress and refuse to load. Take your time and reassure him often, and repeat the longer ride with a buddy to help calm his nerves.

PART II

SAFETY ON
THE GROUND

DEATH TIP
34

Never De-Worm, Vaccinate, Trim Hooves, Or Float A Horse's Teeth.

THE *Myth*

There is no need to vaccinate; it's bad for the horse. Worms are not a problem in your area, and his feet are fine, just fine.

Happily EVER AFTER

Each owner is responsible for their horse's health and preventative care. The number one cause of death in horses is colic. The number one cause of colic is parasites. Certain vaccinations may be needed in different parts of the world, so check with your veterinarian for your region's requirements. However, both hoof and mouth care are a universal Must-Do for any horse owner.

There are many options for treating your horse for parasites, so you will need to research to find what the best method is for you, your horse, and your individual situation. There are many non-toxic homeopathic options available and you may choose this course according to your own findings. Whether you choose western medicine or a homeopathic route, you will need to educate yourself on parasites and their life cycle. Learn to do a fecal exam or have your veterinarian perform as needed to know what parasites to target.

Each owner is responsible for their horse's health and preventative care.

Vaccinations are controversial, and an individual preference so your own education is of utmost importance.

Hoof care is not optional. The old saying, "No feet, no horse," is true. Your whole horse rests on four small hooves. They need to be trimmed and balanced every six to eight weeks. Shoeing him is your choice, but trimming is a must.

Teeth are not optional and are absolutely necessary for a horse to eat, assimilate his food, and survive. A yearly dental check is advisable, and as he ages, the frequency may need to increase. Tooth pain or discomfort can have an effect on the entire body, making him appear lame, causing him to act out or may even cause colic.

TIDBIT
Keeping your horse healthy will require you to study, learn, and determine his health needs.

DEATH TIP 35

Hold The Rope Tightly Near His Chin.

THE Myth

When leading your horse, firmly clutch the lead rope where the snap attaches to the halter, apply constant pressure and drag him along with you.

Happily EVER AFTER

Horses are a lot like cats in that they don't like being restrained or held too tightly, so holding the lead too close to the snap can cause him to panic as he tries to get away.

- Never lead a horse by placing yourself in front, underneath, or behind him. Children especially, must be taught to walk beside and not under a horse.

- Holding the rope too close to the horse's head forces a shorter person to be right under the horse's neck and directly in front of the animal's front legs.

- A horse must use his head and neck for balance, so, if you're hanging on his chin you keep him from being able to keep steady

- His eyes are set to the sides of his head, he can't see directly in front of his nose (especially if you are in front or under him), you may end up tangled in his legs trying to avoid clashing hooves.

Do not wrap the rope around your hand, waist, or arm.

★ TIDBIT

Walk with your horse as you would your best friend, holding the lead comfortably as you would their hand.

- If your horse gets ahead of you, pull his nose toward you. This makes his hindquarters move away from you and decreases the chances of him accidentally kicking you.

- If he spooks and bolts, just let go so you aren't dragged, and watch those back feet as he takes off; in all the excitement, he may buck and kick.

The safest way to lead a horse is to hold the lead rope about twelve inches from the lead snap with your right hand and hold the rest coiled in your left hand. Do not wrap the rope around your hand, waist, or arm. Do not pull the horse along; allow him to walk with you.

Lead a horse from the near side, walking next to him between his head and shoulder. Leading your horse by holding the lead a foot from his chin allows him to see where he is going, and lets him use his head and neck for balance.

DEATH TIP
36

▼

Never Show A Horse You Are Afraid.

THE *Myth*

It's common knowledge: if your horse knows you are afraid, it will end badly because he will take advantage of your fear and ultimately try to kill you. The best solution is to just cowboy up and push through it—no matter how scared you feel.

Happily EVER AFTER

We've all heard this mantra; even children know not to let the horse see their fear. If this were true, it would follow that the main goal and intent of every equine alive is to do harm to humans, and every horse would spend all their time calculating when best to strike.

Here's how it really works: If you are terrified and shaking, crying, screaming, and whining—with your heart racing and your breathing rasping like a chugging locomotive—yes, you will likely have an unpleasant and adrenaline-ridden experience with your horse. Why, you ask? The short answer is simply that a horse is a prey animal. He must be aware of his surroundings and his herdmates at all times. However, if you, his leader, are afraid, he will follow along and be on high alert and ready to run from whatever is causing you distress. If your frightened energy turns you into the scary thing, you've created the makings of a perfect train wreck. This is why learning to control your own emotions will help him as well. Both of you will feel safer.

Fear is not a bad thing or something to avoid. Our fear allows us to sense when our life is in danger, and, in a real emergency, this recognition can keep us out of harm's

Fear is not a bad thing or something to avoid.

way when we need to respond quickly and without thought. It works the same way in the equine world.

The truth is you will never be able to completely hide your emotional state from a horse. What you can do—what you should do—is recognize that your apprehension indicates you are living in a future that hasn't happened yet. Your job is to decide if the fear is real—for instance, if your horse is amped up so high, you feel like you're riding a keg of dynamite and death is imminent—or if it is your own internal and abstract anxiety over something you think might happen.

The trick is to know the difference between when you should walk away and when you need to push through your fear, but not because the horse will intentionally be out to get you if he knows you are afraid. A qualified trainer/instructor can help you tell the difference between the two, but if you don't have a trainer and feel fear, don't ride.

Showing fear to a horse won't help anything, but it doesn't automatically turn him into a killer either. Ride the horse you are on in the moment, and if you are afraid, admit it and get off if you feel staying on is too scary.

THE *Myth*

Stand behind your horse and pick up his tail to begin grooming. Pull a comb through the hairs starting from the top and tugging down to the ends. When you encounter a knot, yank hard because everyone knows that horses can't feel pain in their manes and tails.

Happily EVER AFTER

Horses do have pain receptors (called nociceptors) at the base of their hair follicles just as humans do, and they don't like pain any more than we do. Pulling their hair does hurt them, but horses, like people, have different levels of pain tolerance.

The best way to comb out tangled long tail hair is to first separate the entire tail into four sections. Standing to the side of your horse, pick up one section and begin brushing out the knots at the end nearest the ground. If the hair is particularly knotted, use your fingers to loosen the mats and use a glycerin based product to help make the strands more slippery and easier to separate. Work your way up the tail from the ends to the tail head and take breaks often.

Of course you can walk behind your horse, and you can even stand there, but be careful about pulling hairs while combing his tail and causing him to kick out in response. When horses kick, they kick straight out behind them, not to the side (like a cow does). By standing to the side of a horse, where he can see you, the likelihood of your being in the line of fire is greatly reduced.

Besides being pretty, a horse's hair is important to keep flies at bay.

When washing his tail, follow the same protocol by standing beside the horse's hindquarters. Begin by holding a bucket near the ends of his tail to begin washing. Rinse from the top down, of course.

Besides being pretty, a horse's hair is important to keep flies at bay. The hairs around his ears, fetlocks, eyebrows, and muzzle are essential for him to feel what is around him if he is in a tight spot—don't cut "bangs" or clip his muzzle.

The mane is less sensitive than the tail on most horses, so pulling the mane hairs doesn't bother them as badly. Never stand directly behind the horse for any reason, and especially if you may need to cause him any pain.

53

THE *Myth*

Your horse is lame, but not always. You have had the vet tell you that he's only going to get worse until the day comes he can't walk on his own, let alone be ridden.

You don't want to be stuck with him and you know that if you Bute (give Phenylburazone) him or Ace (give Acepromazine) him (give him painkillers or tranquilizers) he goes pretty well and the lameness is not as noticeable. Better yet, when you drug him, he doesn't have such a sour expression, his teeth don't gnash, and his ears aren't plastered against his head. Really, no one can tell he's uncomfortable, so you'll be able to pass him off as sound and sell him to an unsuspecting novice. Cut your losses and be done with him!

Happily EVER AFTER

Sure, this is not a safety issue in the truest sense; at least not for the seller or the buyer. But for the horse, it can mean death.

Lameness can be masked and even the attending veterinarian may miss the fact the horse is drugged when he/she comes to do the pre-purchase exam. However, once that horse is gone and the new owners see his lameness and have the vet back out for an exam on an un-drugged horse, the truth comes out.

The new owner will be angry, heartbroken, and at a loss as to what to do next. Getting her money back from you isn't likely, and now she's stuck with a horse she can't ride and money spent that she can't get back. She can't sell the horse since he's lame and besides, it's only a matter of time before the horse no longer benefits from the temporary relief he may get from special (expensive) shoes and drugs to keep him somewhat comfortable.

Few people can afford the monetary expense of having an un-rideable horse to care for long-term. For many, the

You may lose money by divulging all the facts regarding your horse, but you'll sleep better knowing you were honest.

★

TIDBIT
Do unto others as you would have done to you. It's that simple.

cost of euthanasia and body disposal is too high after losing the purchase price, and paying the vet bills. In the best outcome, the horse is given to a rescue and they are stuck with the cost of ending his life in an honorable manner. In the worst case, the horse is taken to auction and sold 'as-is'. Many times, the obviously lame are passed over by all but the kill buyers who ship the horses to slaughter where they die a horrible and painful death.

It is never okay to dump a horse on an unsuspecting buyer by lying and drugging an animal. It's not okay to take advantage of a beginner or first time buyer and in the end, it is the horse who suffers.

You may lose money by divulging all the facts regarding your horse, but you'll sleep better knowing you were honest. "Buyer beware" does not excuse any seller from practicing integrity.

DEATH TIP
39

Choose The Veterinarian
Clinic Nearest To Your Barn.

THE *Myth*

The very best vet is the one who can get to your barn the fastest.

TIDBIT

A good veterinarian explains all options regarding the care of your horse and is happy to answer questions in detail—using words you understand.

Happily EVER AFTER

You should like your vet, but that is also not the only reason to choose him or her.

Even before you buy a horse, you will need a veterinarian to help you choose a sound horse and to perform the pre-purchase exam on your chosen mount. If you don't have a veterinarian yet, start looking now, and remember, not all vets are created equal.

Each and every licensed veterinarian went to college, but not all graduated at the top of their class. Fact is some are better practitioners than others. Ask your potential future veterinarian which university they attended and how they ranked. Ask a lot of other horse owners who they use and why. Check with your local Better Business Bureau and any other local organization you are able to utilize.

Do your homework—search for the best match for your horse's needs. You should like your vet, but that is also not the only reason to choose him or her. Here are a few other things to look at when evaluating doctors for your horse:

- How does your horse respond to them?
- Do they seem confident around large animals, or do they have their technician do everything?
- Do they insist upon sedation for even minor procedures?
- Do they walk up and immediately begin "working" or do they take a minute to say hello to your horse?
- If the riding you do places a lot of strain on your horse's joints, does this vet know legs and how to determine lameness issues?
- How long have they been practicing?
- Can you communicate easily with them?
- How available are they?
- What is your first opinion of their character and ethics?

Choose a vet before you need one and be thorough in your evaluation of him or her.

THE *Myth*

Filthy dirty beast! You want a pretty horse that is clean and smells nice so you bathe him with shampoo followed by conditioner so often he begins to smell like a flower garden. You're thorough and pay particular attention to his private areas.

Happily EVER AFTER

Your horse has skin and hair that is best left alone other than daily grooming. If you wash him too often, you will potentially remove essential oils which allows bacteria and fungus to grow and strips his natural defenses against insects and weather. Wetting a horse's hair and skin is fine, but not drying properly can cause fungal infections.

Too much water can damage hooves as well, so be careful not to disrupt nature's balance. Hooves are much like our own fingernails. If we are in water a lot of the time, the nails grow faster, and become weak. Picture your nails when on vacation in a hot, humid area of the world and you'll likely recall having longer nails faster than normal, but as soon as you return to a dry climate, they break easily. The same is true for horse's hooves; they become wet and soft, then dry, brittle and cracked.

If you wash your horse's genital areas too often, you may notice they will start to have irritated skin or infections if you don't rinse properly. Never wash the inside of a mare's vulva, as you may inadvertently introduce bacteria or fungus. It's a good idea to ask your veterinarian to demonstrate how and when to clean your gelding's sheath so you can learn to so properly.

When beginning to wash or rinse your horse, first run water over the feet and legs to get him used to the water and the hose. Spray only when he is comfortable with the water running over his legs, and stop spraying when he stands still, not while he's moving. This teaches him that standing is good and makes future encounters with water easier for both of you.

A wash-rack is an area that has cement or rubber floors to prevent slipping and both hot and cold water are available for bathing a horse. Sometimes, instead of bathing, vacuums are used. Make sure to introduce the vacuum to the horse slowly and in a way that desensitizes him to the sound and feel of it. Do not cross-tie when first introducing the machine and allow him to look at it and touch it before turning it on.

Horses can go their entire lives without a bath if you groom daily, and don't need a sparkling horse in the show ring. First thing he'll do once you've bathed him is roll in the dirt. He knows he needs the dirt and oils for protection.

> Sometimes, instead of bathing, vacuums are used.

TIDBIT
Never spray a horse directly in the face or into his eyes or ears.

THE *Myth* It's a pain to have to clean tack. Besides, dirty, grimy tack works just as well as clean.

★

TIDBIT
Keep in mind that cleaning leather with glycerin soap makes it slippery, so rinse thoroughly.

Happily EVER AFTER

By cleaning your tack thoroughly and regularly, you can inspect each item and you will know if anything is in disrepair. Check to be sure the straps and buckles are still in good working order, and make sure your saddle's tree still intact and not broken or twisted.

With leather tack, a quick wipe down with a damp cloth after every use is sufficient, but once a month, clean thoroughly with saddle soap. The dirtier the leather is, the more the grains of sand and grime can compromise the leather. If any leather goods feel dry, they need to be conditioned using quality saddle oil. Ask at your tack store for recommendations and if you choose Neatsfoot™ oil, be sure to use only the Pure Neatsfoot™ oil, the

Check to be sure the straps and buckles are still in good working order, and make sure your saddle's tree still intact and not broken or twisted.

animal-based product. Petroleum-based products are not kind to leather and can rot linen stitching.

Synthetic tack: Just because your tack isn't made of leather doesn't exempt you from caring for it and cleaning it properly. Pay close attention to where the man-made material straps may have cracked or broken. Wash thoroughly and use the recommended cleaner at least once a month if riding often.

Check metal for rusting, and be sure to dry thoroughly before using on your horse.

Besides looking better, clean tack is more comfortable for you and your horse. Clean your tack regularly; it will last longer, and perform better.

THE *Myth*

Demonstrating your dominance over your horse at all times is the best way to show him who's the boss. If you are the alpha and have his respect, your horse will never be aggressive, assertive, or pushy. He will always wait for, and then follow your every wish and command. Do this right, you will have a horse that will walk through fire, fly over obstacles, and be perfect one hundred percent of the time.

Happily EVER AFTER

> ★ **TIDBIT**
> If you feel your horse is too pushy, examine how you are sending the message to him that he should take over the leadership role.

Most training techniques prescribe that we dominate by using fear and intimidation methods in order to achieve results. The belief is that if not submissive, the horse will begin with small disrespectful behaviors like nudging you with his head, or nipping at your clothes so that he may move up in the 'pecking order'. The presumed expectation is that he will escalate in his badness and most likely kill you dead since you let him dominate you.

In reality, these very behaviors are more a sign of trust and acceptance than disrespect. Watch horses in the wild and you will see the seemingly bottom horse is allowed to interact with the highest ranking member of the herd, even touching him or playing with him.

Dominance amongst horses is observed when there is a competition for resources—food, water, mares. However,

> **Dominance amongst horses is observed when there is a competition for resources—food, water, mares.**

we don't compete for any of their resources; we control them already, so there is no reason for any competition. Teaching the horse to look to you for guidance and then rewarding him is a far superior way to spend time with him and ultimately train him.

It's true that horses like to have a leader to show them what is expected, and they like to know their own place and responsibility within the herd. We do need to be good leaders so the horse will want to follow and comply with our wishes, and we need to learn when and how to discipline. The relationship to strive for with your horse is one of friendship, with mutual respect and love.

DEATH TIP 43

You're Number One!

THE *Myth*

Your comfort and happiness is most important. Don't worry about how your horse feels. Ride alone in unknown areas, on uneven ground, and gallop whenever possible, even if temperatures soar or plummet. If his tack doesn't fit perfectly, it's not a problem. Your biggest concern is how much fun you are having, and that's just how things should be, since you take such good care of your horse.

Happily EVER AFTER

★

TIDBIT

Pain, discomfort, worry, or bad health can cause a horse to act out in negative ways that jeopardize your safety and his.

You have one duty to your horse at all times, every day and everywhere; you must help your horse feel safe.

The trouble is, what you think is harmless and what your horse feels about the situation may be two entirely different things. Remind yourself to think like a horse; base what you do in every situation on what he thinks and feels.

In the wild, a "good" horse, a "successful" horse, is the one that can either get away from or destroy his opponent. This means he reacts first and thinks about what scared him later. He does not take time to evaluate the odds on whether what is scaring him might kill and eat him. It is in his genetics, hardwired into his DNA, to react first. His first reaction will most likely be to get away really fast or kill the killer before it can strike.

Put his needs before your own:

- physically (how he feels about himself and his surroundings)

- mentally (how he thinks and processes his world)

- emotionally (how his mood in the moment can affect his mental and physical responses)

A horse that feels secure, and trusts his human, is less likely to spook, bolt, buck, or rear. Hone your empathetic skills, and you will put your horse's comfort first, which in turn keeps you safe.

In the wild, a "good" horse, a "successful" horse, is the one that can either get away from or destroy his opponent.

DEATH TIP
44
▼

Hook Your Finger In The Metal Halter Ring.

THE *Myth*

On nylon web halters, there are many rings, just pick one, stick your finger through and tug to lead your horse. If it's a knotted rope halter, use the loop below the chin or any other part you can reach.

Happily EVER AFTER

This is a good way to break your finger or get dragged and trampled as you become entangled under your horse. If you attach yourself to any tack item on your horse and he decides to go a direction you hadn't planned, you may not be able to get loose and therefore, could be seriously injured or killed.

If he panics and runs, your own instinct will be to hold on tighter until a split second later, when you realize you need to let go. By then, it's too late; he's gone from zero to thirty so fast, you inadvertently became an entangled accessory that flaps and flounders in desperate attempts to escape. The very best injury to expect in this example would be a broken finger. No need to define the worst case scenario. Never lead your horse without a lead rope; the metal won't 'give', but your finger will.

A great way to teach your horse to lead with good manners is to reward him for keeping his attention on you. He will follow his nose, which follows his mind. This

Never lead your horse without a lead rope; the metal won't 'give', but your finger will.

means that simply, if he wants to be with you, his feet will keep him near and you will walk together happily. If, on the other hand, his attention wanders or he is allowed to graze when he decides to do so, you may find that leading him is not easy or fun.

Keep the rope long enough for him to look around, but short enough to walk next to you, or behind you, if that is your preference. Stay in tune with him and your surroundings and stop periodically to reassure him that he is doing a good job following you.

⋯⋯ ★ ⋯⋯

TIDBIT
Liberty training using positive reinforcement can better your horse's opinion of you and strengthen your bond so he is easier to handle at all times.

THE *Myth*

To tie your horse, use your reins or a rope—up until-now, your perfect steed has always remained still and calm while tied—no matter what he's attached with, or to. Then, suddenly, out of the blue, he pulls back. The colorful purple nylon reins you tied him with don't break. The headstall is the same material and it doesn't break, either. Your horse pulls back harder and yanks until; like a dog playing tug of war; he is sitting back, shaking his head, eyes bulging. Still, nothing gives.

Then you hear a *pop* and he stops struggling.

The *pop* may have been his jaw bone or his neck. Either way, the struggle ends and your horse is dead.

Happily EVER AFTER

Tying with the reins works right up until it doesn't.

Never tie a horse using anything other than a halter and lead rope. Preferably a leather halter and a cotton rope as these natural materials are far more likely to break than nylon. Never tie a horse that is wearing a nylon knotted halter. Although all the current rage, these can cause the most damage as the knots sit over sensitive facial nerves and the ropes themselves are thin and capable of cutting into his flesh. If your horse doesn't actually die, he'll likely end up with nerve damage to his face, jaw or poll.

"Tie to the eye" is an old saying meaning to tie at the horse's eye level, which is whither height or above. Be sure and tie the horse just slightly above his wither-height and leave no more than twelve inches slack so he is unable to get his poll under the rope. When horses feel pressure across the nerves behind their ears, they often panic and rear. If he is tied and can't get away, he may struggle so hard and violently, he ends up sitting on his haunches. Once he falls from this position, he may hang himself, breaking his neck and dying.

Never tie your horse with a non-breakable man-made material.

> Be sure and tie the horse just slightly above his wither-height and leave no more than twelve inches slack so he is unable to get his poll under the rope.

TIDBIT
Your horse's beautiful long neck has the same number of cervical vertebrae as you; seven.

THE *Myth*

You want your horse to back up, and you can force a half-ton animal back by digging in and shoving with all your might.

★

TIDBIT

Horses need to see behind to know it's safe to step backwards; so hold the line long enough that he may turn his head to look behind himself.

Happily EVER AFTER

Standing under any part of a horse is a good way to get hurt. If you are under him, he can't see you. If something comes from behind and scares him, he may leap forward to get away from it, especially when frightened. He won't mean to harm you, but his first response is to think of his own safety.

To step a horse backwards while on the ground, face him and stand to the side of his head and shoulder. Tug gently on the lead by pulling down and back, then release when he steps backward to reward him.

There is a popular method of shaking the lead back and forth so that the snap hits his jaw bone. Though this method works to get the horse to back, it is not respectful to the horse. This technique is good for getting a horse to back away fast and can be used as a quick punishment in case getting the horse to back off quickly is needed. Better to save this technique for emergency situations.

Although horses can see behind themselves, they can't see the ground where they are stepping while backing.

Another popular method entails staring the horse down by looking directly into his eyes to intimidate him. Supposedly, you will mimic a predator and this will send him backwards, away from you. Not true, but using this technique sure could help him see that you are not trustworthy!

Standing under a horse's neck and pushing on his chest usually doesn't work anyway. For some reason, horses will lean against you instead of backing up.

Although horses can see behind themselves, they can't see the ground where they are stepping while backing. Sometimes this makes it difficult to unload them from a straight load trailer, so practice using a step to help give him confidence.

DEATH TIP
47

Horses Are Tough And Can Take Care Of Themselves.

THE *Myth*

Horses do not need any extra care. Just give them a pasture and a creek and they'll be fine. Wild horses live without all the babying and fussing, so your horse can too.

★
TIDBIT
Shelter is a necessity for horses in all climates. When it is rainy or windy, their natural hair-defense is quite inefficient.

Happily EVER AFTER

Horse owners are responsible for their horse's health and well-being; period. Depending upon where you live and what your weather conditions are, you will need to provide whatever keeps your horse healthiest.

In very cold climates, for example, your horse may need his water heated in the winter. Horses tend to not drink enough water when it is cold if their water is also near freezing temperature. The water simply needs to be above freezing and not hot.

Where the climate is hot and humid, the horse may not be able to sufficiently cool his body temperature sufficiently if he is ridden hard and for long periods of time during the heat of the day. Electrolyte balance is important in all cases and drinking enough water is critical for the body to function at optimum capacity.

Providing salt is an important supplement and should be offered as free choice for all horses in all climates. The correct salt to give horses is equally critical. If you have

Providing salt is an important supplement and should be offered as free choice for all horses in all climates.

ever been licked by a cat or a cow, you'll have noticed the roughness of their tongues. Conversely, a horse's tongue is soft and smooth. It is the smoothness of the tongue that tells us to offer him a soft salt or loose salt. The big white, red and yellow fifty-pound salt blocks are too dense for horses to lick easily. Sure, they are better than nothing, but explore using a loose salt or Himalayan rock salt—both are easier for the horse to consume. The Himalayan salt can be purchased in handy smaller sizes that are pre-drilled and can be hung by a thick string. This keeps them from melting in the rain and it also allows the salt to stay cleaner as it is not at ground level.

A lot of calories and energy is used to maintain body temperature; both in hot and cold weather. Be sure to research and ask your vet how best to feed your horse for the environment he lives in and offer the horse enough quality food, fresh water and good salt to help him thrive.

Tie Your Horse With A Rope Around His Neck While You Bridle Him.

THE *Myth*

Your horse is saddled, ready to go and it's time to put the bridle on and get going. First, take the halter off, then re-buckle or tie it around his neck before leaving him to fetch your bridle. You've done it this way for years and it's always been fine, so you know this is a safe practice.

Happily EVER AFTER

Your horse stands there, but then realizes there is a sprig of hay just out of reach. As he stretches his nose to get it, he feels the halter around his neck and violently pulls back against the pressure. Since the halter is buckled around his neck and the lead is tied tightly and he pulls back, you cannot untie him fast enough to save him from breaking his neck or cutting his legs on the metal trailer as he thrashes about trying to get free. It's that clear and that simple. Do not do this.

If you must tie the halter around the neck, hold the lead rope in your hand, or lay it over your arm as you bridle him. That way, if he pulls, you can just walk forward with him until you can stop him.

> ♆
> **Never tie a horse by attaching him with something secured around his neck, especially if it can tighten and choke him.**

Never bridle a tied horse unless you are putting the bridle over the halter, and even then you're taking a chance if he spooks or pulls back.

Never tie a horse by attaching him with something secured around his neck, especially if it can tighten and choke him. If a horse has a noose around his neck and sits back, there is a good chance the result will be a broken neck.

Train your horse to look for the bridle by tipping his head to your abdomen and giving him a reward—a pat or a treat—before bridling him. If his head is turned toward you, he will focus on your actions and the task at hand rather than getting away from you. Make it fun!

TIDBIT
Always tie your horse with a quick-release knot.

THE *Myth*

Leave the halter on at all times; he's easier to catch that way. Horses can be rough on tack, so choose a durable, flat nylon halter, or even better, a knotted rope one.

★

TIDBIT

A horse can catch his hoof in the halter if he scratches his head with a hind foot; if he's shod, he may break his leg or neck or both.

Happily EVER AFTER

It does seem like not a bad idea to leave the halter on your horse, after all, dogs wear collars all the time, but horses seem to have a way of getting hurt no matter how safe we make their environment. A simple fence post or a tree branch can snag his halter and send him into a blind panic that causes him serious physical damage or even death. Knotted rope halters hang loosely on the horse's head, and are even more likely to catch on things. Never leave a halter on the horse while he is loose and unattended.

Some people think they need to leave a halter on a horse because they can't catch him, but since this doesn't fix the problem, it avoids the need to train and it is not a great idea long-term. If you can't catch your horse, the answer is to train him to not only be caught, but to come when you call him. If needed, keep him in a small area until you are certain he understands the lesson, and keep a breakaway halter on him during this time.

Take your time and teach him to come to you, but do not 'catch' him. Instead, offer a treat or a pat and then walk away. Come back in a few minutes and call him again,

If an item must be left on him full-time, such as a halter, cribbing collar, blanket, it needs to be breakable.

reward as you did before and then once more, leave. Repeat this as many times as it takes for him to come to you on command when you call him, reach out to pet him on the neck, not the face. Reward, leave, and repeat. Build up in small increments to being able to call him, have him lower his head and see the rope without him worrying. You may want to walk around and let him follow you a few times as well. But, until he is willing to stand quietly, do not grab the halter, or throw a rope over his neck. When he is consistently standing and is soft-eyed and comfortable, with a low head, introduce another halter while he is still wearing the first one. Do not be intent on haltering him the first time, but teach him to lower his head and put his nose into the nosepiece on his own. Reward often. Keep the lessons short, fun and before you know it, you will have an easily caught horse!

If an item must be left on him full-time, such as a halter, cribbing collar, blanket, it needs to be breakable. Leather is best and there are halters made specifically to break away in case of entanglement, but ideally, the horse should be 'naked'.

Keeping your horse safe—even from himself—is a primary concern. Take the halter off!

THE *Myth*

One day, out of the clear blue, your horse won't cross the exact same obstacle he has many times in the past—a creek, a bridge, the yellow line in the road, a curb, or even a bush. You kick him, he balks. You kick harder, his head raises, his tail swishes and he stomps his feet in place; but he doesn't budge. You are angry, and you hit him with the ends of your reins. He bucks and you fall off. You aren't physically hurt, but your feelings are. You catch him and ask him why he acts like that, then demand why he doesn't take care of you the way you take care of him.

Expect him to behave as soon as you point out all you do for him. After all, that's the deal you made, isn't it?

Happily EVER AFTER

A horse does not understand, care, or even think about the fact you take care of him and he should therefore be indebted to you. He has no concept of money, or the amount you spend on his well-being. He does not buy, sell, barter, or trade. He has no bank account and does not keep a tab on who owes him or who he might owe. You have a never-ending debt to your horse, but he is not indebted to you. He isn't capable of understanding the concept of indebtedness.

More important than your need to be repaid, is your responsibility to figure out why he suddenly doesn't do as you ask. Abrupt changes in behavior often indicate a physical problem rather than a training issue. If you are sure he is sound and comfortable, with properly fitted tack, ask yourself where the pot holes in his training may be and if you are able to do the schooling needed. If you can't tell, hire a qualified trainer to help you.

You have a never-ending debt to your horse, but he is not indebted to you.

Your debt to your horse is to provide him everything he needs physically, emotionally and mentally. His debt to you is nonexistent. Your horse is not obliged to take care of you.

TIDBIT
Horses are kind and gentle by nature, but this doesn't mean that their job is to take care of us.

THE *Myth*

You bought a horse, your neighbor has horses, and she says she'll be your trainer. She advises on tack, training methods and even rides your horse for you. Bonus—she doesn't even charge you!

★

TIDBIT
The definition of a
non-professional is
'amateur'.

Happily EVER AFTER

It can be quite attractive having a neighbor who appears to know more than you do offer to train you and your horse; plus, it's cheaper and easier than hiring a professional. No hauling, no boarding, and besides, you trust your neighbor.

The downside of this plan is that instead of her having the training and experience of working with hundreds of horses, the neighbor might have only a few under her belt. Sure, that's more than you can claim, but it doesn't make her a pro. This is one of those situations where you get what you pay for and you must decide if it's worth the risk.

Horses are different than a vehicle needing work where any mechanic familiar with your model can fix the problem. Each horse is a unique individual and may need help in a way your neighbor just isn't capable of doing. If you want the job done right, hire the right person; one who has the qualifications needed to teach your horse what he needs to know.

A horse is trained one time only, and after that, it's re-training, which takes two or three times longer than training.

Training is not something everyone knows how to do correctly for each horse and even professionals struggle with some cases; an amateur won't have the necessary skills to help a needful horse correctly. It takes time and experience along with patience, but even more importantly, a trainer needs to have a sense of empathy. Just because someone owns horses, says they have trained many and claims they can help you, doesn't mean it's a good idea.

A horse is trained one time only, and after that, it's re-training, which takes two or three times longer than training. In the end, any funds saved by getting free help will likely be spent doubly in retraining or your own medical bills.

Being a good neighbor doesn't qualify a person as a professional horse trainer. You wouldn't let your plumber work on your car just because he lives next door and drives a car himself, would you?

DEATH TIP

52

▼

When Saddling, Cinch From Front To Back. Don't Forget The Breast Collar.

THE *Myth*

Put the saddle on the horse, snap the breast collar on to hold it steady, and then cinch the girth up tight before buckling the back cinch. You could also start at the back cinch and work forward since that makes sense too.

Happily EVER AFTER

Saddling is a precise task that needs to be done correctly to keep both you and your horse safe. If you ride English, you set the saddle, make sure the pad is smooth and even on all sides, and tighten the girth. If you use a breastplate, you'll buckle that up after the saddle is on.

But if you ride Western, you will need to put the pad on correctly; heft the saddle onto the horse without throwing it at him (thereby spooking him or hitting him with a wayward stirrup), and then start cinching him up.

A back cinch and breast collar are needed if you are roping, riding up and down steep hills, or your saddle tends to slip, but otherwise they are cumbersome weight added to your horse's burden. A properly fitted saddle should not move around a lot, so if this is happening, have a professional saddle fitter or trainer look at it and evaluate. Be sure and choose the proper length girth or cinch by measuring where the rings or buckles will lie against the horse's sides, and adjust it by centering the D ring facing forward evenly between the front legs.

The proper order of cinching up a Western saddle with front and back cinches and a breast collar is as follows:

- Once the horse is groomed and the pad is set correctly over his withers and is even on both sides, set the saddle on the horse without throwing it at him.

- Begin with the front cinch, and tighten it just enough so that the saddle won't fall off if the horse moves.

- Connect the breastplate by bringing it across the horse's chest and buckling it to the near side of the saddle's D ring.

- Snap the short strap that is hanging between the horse's front legs to the D ring on the front cinch.

- Tighten the back cinch tight enough so that if he was to kick at a fly, he wouldn't tangle himself in the cinch with his hind foot, but don't make it so tight that it becomes a bucking strap.

- Go back to the front cinch and tighten it a little bit at a time until it is as snug as you desire.

- Remember to check the skin behind his elbow for wrinkles so that he doesn't get galled.

- A narrow leather breast collar can rub and cut into a horse's shoulders, so choose a wide, flat one or use a fleece sleeve to prevent chafing.

Saddling is a precise task that needs to be done correctly to keep both you and your horse safe.

DEATH TIP

53

▼

Just Because He/She Said They Were A Trainer, Doesn't Mean They Are.

THE *Myth*

They posted an ad on the bulletin board at the feed store and that is proof enough that they must know what they're doing. Besides, they are close to you and your neighbor approves.

Happily EVER AFTER

Your trainer must have the ability to help both you and your horse continue learning while increasing the level of communication between you. Remember, every day across the world, someone who loves horses and wants to work with them, declares themselves as a trainer. Horse training isn't a profession where earning a college degree or holding a license means a person is qualified to train. Simply, no one can learn to train by sitting in a classroom, or watching videos or reading books, or attending clinics until they earn a certificate. Even having a certificate from another person does not make the recipient a qualified trainer; rather, it means money has been paid, lessons have been taken and a certificate was earned.

Horses are alive, with minds, emotions and memories combined with genetic material that makes each one react differently in the same exact same situation. There is no formula, no magic protocol, and no one person who can teach anyone what to do in every situation. This knowledge is only gained over years and from the horses themselves.

The wrong trainer can cause irrevocable damage in a very short time; a bad half-hour session can ruin the horse. Since there is no way to be sure that the self-proclaimed trainer truly is qualified and able, you must take responsibility for gathering the information needed to ensure you chose correctly. Watch a few lessons and training sessions as they work with their client's horses. Ask questions about their past experience and their training philosophy. Of course their rates are important, but the least or even the most expensive is not always the right fit. For example, if you want to have a young horse started, ask how many other horses they've trained and what methods they use; then watch them work with at least three different horses and observe three different riding lessons. If you don't like what you see, keep looking.

Be cautious and skeptical. Ask around and dig to find a trainer's reputation. Talk to your veterinarian and your farrier for advice when looking for someone to help you and your horse. Your trainer must have the knowledge and experience to help you develop a deep understanding of your horse's highest mental, physical, and emotional potential.

There is no formula, no magic protocol, and no one person who can teach anyone what to do in every situation.

> ### ⭐ TIDBIT
>
> A good trainer coaches both you and your horse to become the best team possible while incorporating a sense of humor, a sense of integrity and a lot of empathy.

DEATH TIP

54

Let Your Farrier Work In The Corral Within The Loose Herd.

THE *Myth*

Your horses are so well-behaved; your farrier could do the work on one horse in their paddock while the other herd members are just hanging out with her while she works.

Happily EVER AFTER

Although it seems a fine plan, horses are horses first, and that means that if they get excited or scared of something, they will move. The other herd members may react, and the animal the farrier is working on will also respond.

If the farrier is in the middle of nailing on a shoe and the horse pulls away quickly, she may get cut very badly by unfinished nails.

A herd milling about near a working farrier may accidentally or purposefully bump into the horse being trimmed or shod. Herd dynamics may cause the horse that has his foot held by the farrier to jump, hop, or pull away as he tries to avoid getting bitten or kicked by a herd member intent on making him move out of the way.

Sometimes horses that are loose in a paddock bite at the farrier's tools, pockets, or chinks. If a loose horse picks up a heavy metal tool and tosses it, that tool may hit the farrier, the horse being worked on, or another herd member. As the tool is carried around or flung by that horse, the metal could break his tooth or teeth.

The job of the handler is to protect the farrier from any potential harm while work is in progress. This means that when the farrier is working, the handler must pay full attention and respond accordingly to any potential hazard that comes up.

The job of the handler is to protect the farrier from any potential harm while work is in progress.

DEATH
TIP

55

When Turned Out To Their
Larger Paddocks Or Pastures,
Horses Are Safe.

THE *Myth*

There's no need to worry about objects in your horse's living quarters—don't trim tree branches or worry about other things in a horse's turnout area or pasture. They know not to run into things, so why bother with creating extra work for yourself?

Happily EVER AFTER

Most horse owners agree on a simple truth: if a horse can get hurt on something, he will. People joke about bubble wrapping their horse to prevent silly, yet costly injuries, but the truth is, it would be nice to keep him safe at all times, and it is every horse owner's desire to avoid unexpected vet bills.

Help keep him safe by locating each and every potential hazard in his pasture or turnout area and then removing them one by one. Low-hanging branches are often overlooked, but they can gouge out an eye or tear his skin deeply. "Low hanging" means about twelve to fifteen feet from the ground. This is because if a horse rears, he can inadvertently hit his head or eye. So cut the branches off flush to the tree's trunk at least that high.

Check the area for rocks, wire, holes in the ground, and any

> Low-hanging branches are often overlooked, but they can gouge out an eye or tear his skin deeply.

other obstacle or hazardous thing you can find. This can include items made of metal, wood, stone, cement, rope, or plastic. Look for any sharp edges along your barn, the fence, and gates. Check for and eliminate any protruding nails, bolts, wire, or anything he can cut himself on, even if you think he can't possible reach it. He can, and he will.

Parked vehicles or trailers within your horse's turnout area are potential hazards for your horse. Best-case incident: the paint gets scraped by equine teeth. Worst-case incident: the horse gets mangled by sharp metal.

Children's toys, dog toys, and other human items belong in the playroom, and equine toys should be removed when the horse is unsupervised. Even rubber balls can cause him to be injured or killed if he rolls over them and lands on his neck.

Clearing debris, junk, or anything other than the horse, the dirt, and his fencing and barn will not ensure his safety 100 percent, but it sure will help him stay out of harm's way easier.

THE *Myth*

After a month of your horse being in training, expect to pick up a perfect working model. While your horse is at the trainer's you don't need to check on his progress, or participate in his lessons—you can just pick up the 'fixed' horse at the end of the month. You do not need to communicate with the trainer, or learn anything new. You know how to ride; it's the horse with the problem, and a month is plenty of time to fix him.

Happily EVER AFTER

People sometimes assume that taking their horse to a trainer is exactly like taking their car into the shop. Drop it off, and then pick up a repaired version. However, horses aren't machines and usually, they aren't broken. So while you can drop a vehicle off with a guy and forget about how he repairs the apparatus, you will benefit most by keeping in the loop with both your trainer and with your horse.

When your horse goes into training, he will learn how to do what you want him to do. If you are not participating in learning the same lessons, you will not have the tools you need to effectively communicate with him. In a sense, he will be speaking a different language than you. Be involved with your horse's training—you need to understand and learn what he learns so you can communicate with him effectively. Horses respond best when cues are consistent, and you must go through the same training so you both know the same cues.

Horses are not broken machines that need fixing, but your way of communicating with each other may need a refresher course. This can take time for both of you to unlearn bad habits.

Proper training takes years, not days to complete and quick-fix methods do not result in a trained horse. He must learn how to respond as you like, not simply become robotic in his reaction to stimuli. In order to learn how to learn, he must be taught how to handle his own emotions.

Proper training takes years, not days to complete and quick-fix methods do not result in a trained horse.

TIDBIT
Flooding (exposing
animal to frightful
stimuli with no release)
is often the method
of 'Fast Training'
and often results in
a shutdown, broken-
spirited horse.

DEATH TIP

57

You Don't Need To Comply With Your Trainer's Instruction.

THE Myth

There is no need to obey all that your trainer tells you. She is full of herself and doesn't know your horse as well as you do, so she can't possibly know how best to get through to him.

Happily EVER AFTER

Different from arguing, noncompliance is the blatant ignoring of all instruction you've paid for. Sometimes you ignore your trainer during a lesson and other times you just blow her off once she's gone; either way disregarding the instruction is not helpful to you or your horse.

This is flagrant disregard for the professionals' opinion and advice, and is disrespectful, too. If you don't want the instruction you paid for, why bother hiring a trainer? If you find yourself thinking you are a better trainer than the person you hired, either find someone you will respect enough to listen to, or complete the job yourself.

When you hire a qualified professional, it is important to follow their advice and learn how to better communicate with your horse. If you find the teachings don't work for you, try another trainer until things begin to click for you and your horse.

Noncompliance is not the answer if you do not agree with the instruction, talk to your trainer, and get clarification. Communication between you and your trainer is essential in order for you to be able to connect with your horse.

Noncompliance is not the answer if you do not agree with the instruction, talk to your trainer, and get clarification.

TIDBIT
Noncompliance is like filling a prescription, choosing not to take the medicine, and then blaming the doctor for not helping you.

THE *Myth*

Why bend over to wrap your horse's legs? So much easier to sit next to his leg in the barn aisle and comfortably work.

⭐ TIDBIT

Never use elasticized bandaging material on the horse's tail, and use caution when applying on legs as it can easily be pulled too tightly.

Happily EVER AFTER

Do not ever sit under your horse. Seems like a no-brainer, but it's surprising how many people do sit under their horse and expect all to end well. Here is why you should never do this:

- If sitting, you cannot get out of the way of a 1,100 pound fast-moving animal quickly enough to avoid being trampled.

- If he gets scared of anything—a sound, sight, touch or smell, he will likely move before thinking.

- Your horse can't see under himself, so he cannot know where you are exactly.

- It's not his job to protect you and keep you safe.

- No matter how trustworthy your horse is, he is a horse first and reacts accordingly.

- You cannot predict the future, which means anything can happen and your reaction time is never as fast as his.

- Even if all he does is kick at a fly tickling his tummy, the likelihood of you being nailed is high.

- While wrapping your horse, be aware that your hair may feel like a fly on his side and he may kick at the nuisance.

- If he does kick at anything and you are sitting on the ground, his back hoof will be in line with your head.

- Stamping a front foot to avoid the bandage itself can end in a broken leg for you if he lands on it.

When only one leg is wrapped, always support the opposite leg with a bandage as well.

To wrap a horse's legs always face him, squat so you can move out of his way quickly. Be sure his legs and the bandaging material are clean and dry. Use the correct type of padding and wrap for the intended purpose and always wrap from top to bottom and lay the wrap in a consistently smooth manner.

Putting too much torque on a wrap can cause decreased blood flow and work like a tourniquet, so it's important to use the proper tension when wrapping so you don't cut off his circulation.

When only one leg is wrapped, always support the opposite leg with a bandage as well. Your horse will stand heavier on the 'good' leg and it too, will eventually get sore, so extra support on that leg is a good idea. Plus, for some unknown reason, some horses will gnaw and worry over one bandage, but will leave both alone if there are two. Maybe it has to do with his feeling balanced?

THE *Myth*

Say your horse won't cross a puddle or get into a horse trailer. Just get behind him and wave a plastic bag or a whip or make a loud noise. We've all heard the saying that if the place you want him to go looks better than the place he is, he'll want to be there, so it must work.

Happily EVER AFTER

This approach may work and a lot of trainers subscribe to this method, but the question to ask is, will your horse learn new tasks if in any emotional state other than trust?

Consider when you first learned to dive off a spring board into a pool; did someone scare you into leaping off and into the water head-first? Or, while learning to ski downhill, as you stood fearfully at the top of the mountain, did someone clap their hands and then shove you into a fast free-fall careen to the bottom? If these scenarios played out, would you ever want to dive or ski again?

Horses are no different. Fear is not a good motivator, even though it does serve to accomplish a set goal quickly and will work the first time or even the first few times. The thing is, just like everything Horse, it works right up until

it doesn't and then you need even more time to train properly—to first undo the fear and apprehension and then to retrain properly using love and patience.

Fear is not a good motivator, even though it does serve to accomplish a set goal quickly and will work the first time or even the first few times.

Better to have no time constraints and to have a calm, relaxed attitude to get the horse to do as you wish. Given time and patience, your horse will learn that you are trustworthy and the new event or place will not kill him. Make it fun for him and remember he thinks in terms of keeping himself safe and trusting you to be a good leader.

Patience, guidance, and good communication skills are your keys to the horse kingdom. Using fear tactics to train is not truly teaching. Training through the use of fear or pain forces the horse choose between two evils and moves him out of Trust and into Fear.

TIDBIT
Training using fear tactics works right up until he is more afraid of something other than you.

While Mucking, Wear A Headset, Dance With The Rake, And Make It Fun!

THE *Myth*  Mucking the corral or cleaning his stall is a daily chore, and you get bored, so why not have some fun to ease the monotony of it all?

★

TIDBIT
A radio turned up loudly can mask some sounds like leaves, pine needles, or ice on the roof and can actually help your horse feel safer.

Happily EVER AFTER

The usual things matter here, like remembering that erratic movements, loud singing (after all, singing and dancing go together!), and flying rakes can scare a horse, and it's your job to keep him feeling safe. Wearing headphones may be entertaining for you, but they also block out other sounds, such as your horse suddenly bolting; you wouldn't hear him coming at full throttle. The flip side is that you shouldn't be wary or walk around cautiously like you are afraid of everything either.

Mucking time can become a very good training time, and you'll do it at least once a day if you are a conscientious horsekeeper. Conditioning and desensitizing your horse to activities you enjoy such as singing and dancing, are good practices. He will become used to your fun-loving ways, though he may want to join you. This is something to beware of because if your 1,100 pound friend decides he should dance with you, he may not be able keep from running over you or becoming so boisterous in his exuberant celebration that he kicks out in joyful dancing glee. This doesn't mean he intended to cause you any harm, but the end result may be disastrous, especially when you include the rogue rake and innocent wheelbarrow that go flying at the same time you do.

> ♘ Mucking time can become a very good training time, and you'll do it at least once a day if you are a conscientious horsekeeper.

Also, remember that if you want a calm, soft-eyed, low-headed horse, you need to convey that same mood to him at all times. Instead of bringing high energy into his world, use your corral-cleaning moments to center and ground yourself and your horse. Being in the moment together is critical for you both to increase your trust of each other. Calm begets calm and keeps everyone happy and secure.

Sadly, if you don't know your horse well, you may not know his past experiences regarding rakes. Many people think that getting a horse to move away from them by poking him with the sharp tines of a manure fork is fine, but it can teach them to fear the rake; especially if it is raised. Your dancing, singing and manure rake flinging may scare him badly enough that he begins to fear you at all times. Some horses learn to kick at the rake, so during your first time cleaning his living quarters, you may want to tie him so that you can keep yourself out of harm's way while you evaluate his opinion of your mucking techniques.

THE *Myth*

You follow the same routine every day, and your horse knows the drill. Blanketing your horse is a great example of how we may take things for granted with our horse in doing some mundane chore day after day. You take the blankets off every morning and put them on every afternoon, so they each know what's coming and when. No big deal, right?

TIDBIT
Use the proper weight of blanket for the weather conditions to keep your horse at the correct temperature.

Happily EVER AFTER

Just because you always put the blanket on and off in the same manner at the same time every day doesn't exempt you from being safe at all times.

Many people blanket their horses by putting the entire blanket on over the head. This saves the extra step of buckling the front closure and speeds things along. These same people also take the blanket off in the morning by unbuckling the belly and leg straps and hauling the blanket off over the head. As long as the horse is conditioned to this method, sometimes, most times, it works great. Right up until it doesn't, and then the train wreck can be deadly for either your horse or you.

The safest way to blanket and unblanket is to halter and tie your horse before beginning. Be sure he is clean and dry and check the blanket itself for dirt, debris, wet spots, and broken straps and buckles. Unbuckle every single buckle. Fold the blanket so you are able to set it gently on his back after he has smelled and inspected it. Then proceed in the following order: From front to back, begin buckling. Start with the front closure, then either skip to the rear leg straps, or just work your way back by

The safest way to blanket and unblanket is to halter and tie your horse before beginning.

doing the belly straps next, and end with the leg straps. By doing the front closure, then the back legs, the blanket is securely on in case the horse gets loose and runs, and the blanket should not slip to one side due to leg straps holding it on. Remove it in the opposite order that you put it on.

If you choose to blanket your herd while each horse is at liberty, remember to pay attention to the horse you are working on, as well as the other herd members. If the horses are standing near one another and you throw the blanket over a back, and a strap or buckle accidentally hits the horse standing near the one you are blanketing, a rocketing herd may result. If the horse you are blanketing takes off with the others and the blanket falls to the side, he may trip and seriously injure himself.

If the horse that got hit by the strap retaliates, your horse may respond by kicking or biting at him and get you instead. Even though he knew you were there, he might not have known that another horse would be attacking him and his response may be instantaneous.

The safest way to blanket and unblanket is to remove each horse from the herd, and halter, tie, and blanket that horse while taking your time and being precise. This is one death tip that few heed, but it's one that is critical.

THE *Myth*

Your horse is fine, and he is always ready for anything you want to do with him. He doesn't have the facial muscles to show any specific expressions that would indicate his mood anyway. As long as his ears are forward, his eyes are bright, and he is standing, he's good to go.

Happily EVER AFTER

Horses use a mixture of body-language stances and facial expressions to express their thoughts and feelings. Being familiar with most horses' overall happy general appearance, you will easily spot any possible problems he may be experiencing.

Most horses, when happy and healthy, tend to be aware of their surroundings but not overly concerned about anything. They appear calm and relaxed with happy expressions and active ears. Their tails will swish periodically, but not to an extreme degree. Their feet will not drag, and their heads will be at a happy elevation—not too high, and not hanging to the ground. Unless the horse is resting or sleeping, the lower lip is not drooping; nor is it tight with wrinkles. Wrinkles around his lips, nostrils, and ears also show you he is not feeling well.

If you notice your horse has his eyes squeezed tightly enough to create wrinkles above or below his socket, this is an indication of pain. Check his eyes for any debris,

> ⊔
>
> **Horses use a mixture of body-language stances and facial expressions to express their thoughts and feelings.**

cuts, or discharge, and if you see any of the above, a call to the vet is necessary.

A healthy and happy horse has nostrils that are even and balanced when you look at him from the front. A raised nostril tells you he may be in pain. If either or both nostrils are flared, check his pulse and respiration since this indicates he is breathing rapidly and maybe with difficulty. Since we are talking about nostrils, check for any discharge. Anything other than clear and runny fluid is a sign that he is sick, and a call to the vet is necessary.

His tail should hang straight down, and if he's holding it up and to one side, this may indicate an upset tummy. Check for signs of loose stool, and check his living quarters for proof he has been defecating. If he is "wagging" his tail quickly, he is distressed. Watch for him to bite his sides or lay down to roll—all of these are signs of colic.

DEATH TIP
63

Don't Worry About
Doing Things Correctly.

THE *Myth*

You know how to do it right, but why bother? It's okay to take a shortcut every once in a while. Go ahead and crawl under your horse, or tie him with the reins to a corral panel, or ride double; heck with worrying about getting hurt or hurting your horse.

Happily EVER AFTER

★

TIDBIT
The point of doing things the right way helps ensure your and your horse's safety.

You will 'get away' with shortcuts and not doing things safely right up until your luck runs out and you find yourself paying the proverbial piper.

Each time we are in the presence of a half-ton, fear-driven animal, it is to our own benefit to think about safety first. Thinking like a horse is critical to keep him feeling safe, which in turn, keeps you out of danger. When working with, or even just standing near a horse, everything must be done in a specific manner so that the horse is comfortable and safe.

Get in the habit of performing each task in the same way, every time, and your horse knows exactly what to expect. This keeps him feeling secure and ultimately, keeps you from being injured. Repetition instills confidence

in your horse and yourself as everyone involved knows what to expect. Practice and repetition are comforting to horses and people.

When the unexpected happens, most of us and our horses react physically by flooding the system with adrenaline. Doing things in a concise and logical manner helps keep everyone involved in a calm state of mind.

Shortcuts are best avoided as they are most desired when we are rushing. Fast movements can cause horses to be afraid even if there is nothing obviously scary to be seen and often, the response is to move quickly, just as you are.

Each time we are in the presence of a half-ton, fear-driven animal, it is to our own benefit to think about safety first.

THE *Myth*

The crud in your horse's feet will fall out as you ride. No need to pick his hooves. After all, wild horses do just fine on their own; why can't yours?

Happily EVER AFTER

The grooves of the frog enable all kinds of things to get stuck and can allow bacteria and fungus to do serious damage. Removing all superfluous junk helps your horse's frog do its job more efficiently.

Cleaning your horse's hooves will get out any rocks or pebbles and keep him comfortable as you ride, or as he grazes during the day. Daily picking of his hooves also lets you check for any problems he may have with his feet. Taking these precautions will keep him comfortable and sound.

When picking a horse's feet, always stand very near him facing his rear, and run your hand down his leg to the fetlock. Tap or gently squeeze to let him know you want him to bend his leg. Hold the coronary band and firmly, but carefully follow the grooves of his frogs to loosen and debris and gravel.

★

TIDBIT
There are no muscles below the knee and hock of a horse, so the frog acts as a pump sending blood back up the leg each time he steps.

Severe cases of thrush can cause lameness, so it's good to keep your horse's feet clean.

If your horse has deep clefts or narrow, contracted heels, he is more at risk of developing thrush; a bacterial infection caused by dirty and wet or muddy living conditions. Severe cases of thrush can cause lameness, so it's good to keep your horse's feet clean. It's easy enough to treat; a mixture of tea-tree oil and water will remedy the situation most times, and there are commercial concoctions available at any tack store. Clean feet are happy feet.

DEATH TIP
65

Horses In A Pasture Are
The Perfect Photo Op.

THE *Myth*

You're driving through the countryside and see some horses in a meadow, stop the car, call the horses to you, and set your child on top of the fence so you can take some pictures. The horses seem really nice and there's no one around, so you climb the fence and set your toddler on top of the prettiest spotted one, and then step back to take a picture.

Another option is to let your child run to the horses, while you take as many photos as possible before someone sees you.

Happily EVER AFTER

Yes, horses are pretty animals and yes, having a picture of your children with them in a lovely pasture seems a good idea. It is not. The horses are not yours. The property is not yours. The fence is there for a couple of reasons; to keep the horses contained, and to keep you out.

Horses, like dogs, should never be approached without permission. Never assume any horse is trained or willing to stand for you to take a picture. Never approach someone else's horse without first getting permission. Never allow a child to enter a pasture, paddock, or barn to run and shout as they call the pretty horsey to come to her.

Horses feel the emotions and energy of others around them; even other species and yes, even people. When a child is excited, the horse feels the excitement and may react in a way that could cause injury to your child. The high-pitch of children's voices can be alarming to horses. Even the gentlest horse can spook or alternatively, be too comfortable and push his nose at the child and hurt her. Horses in a meadow are not there for you to approach just because you feel like it.

> Even the gentlest horse can spook or alternatively, be too comfortable and push his nose at the child and hurt her.

TIDBIT

Respect other people, their property, and their animals and ask permission before touching any horse.

THE *Myth*

Tie the knot tightly—any kind of knot will do. It doesn't matter how you tie a horse, as long as it keeps him where you want him.

★
TIDBIT
Many horses learn to untie themselves so use a knot he can't figure out and teach him to keep his mouth off the rope!

Happily EVER AFTER

Tying a knot is easy enough and tying a horse to something is nothing to be too concerned about; just loop the rope around the stationary object and tie any old knot you can, and you're done. This works right up until your horse pulls back tightening the knot so that it can never be untied and you must cut the rope.

Besides losing the now-cut and ruined rope, if your horse does pull back, something has to give—either the rope, the thing your horse is tied to, or the horse himself. It is imperative to have a knot you are able to release so he doesn't hang himself or break his neck.

A quick release knot is the best kind to use, so if you only learn one good knot, make it that one. Remember to tie the horse at his withers height or above in case you can't release him fast enough to prevent him from hanging himself.

When tying the knot, remember to keep your fingers out of any loops made by the rope.

When tying the knot, remember to keep your fingers out of any loops made by the rope. Nothing worse than being in the middle of knotting and the horse resists by pulling back and you find you are now sporting a couple of broken fingers. Have an experienced trainer teach you which knot is best and easiest to use. Or, this may be a good reason to take a sailing lesson and learn some good nautical knots.

Keep a knife nearby at all times. If your horse does pull back tightening the knot so that you can't untie it, have a knife handy so you can cut the rope. In an emergency, cutting through cotton is easier and faster than cutting through nylon, so using cotton ropes just makes good sense.

PART III

SAFETY IN
THE SADDLE

THE *Myth*

You've never landed on your head, so why bother with a hard hat? Those are for sissies, and, besides, the helmet makes your head sweat and when you take the thing off, you are left with ugly hat hair. So unattractive!

Happily EVER AFTER

Most people prefer not to wear head protection, but injuring your brain can happen more easily than you might expect, and wearing a helmet is the only protection you have. Most trainers and almost all boarding facilities make wearing a helmet mandatory for anyone under eighteen years of age, but doesn't it make sense that older people should protect themselves, too?

People often say, "It's just not cool to wear a helmet, and it shows that I'm just learning." The thing is, your likelihood of falling off as you learn is a distinct probability and having your head covered with the correct protection is a smart precaution.

So many ways to get hurt, such as falling off and landing on, or simply hitting your head. If you are wearing a hard hat specifically made for horseback riding, you might end up with a headache, but nothing else.

The good news is that the heavy helmet of yesteryear is now lightweight, vented and attractive. Many different options and colors are available, but be sure and choose a good one. You can spend $600 on a helmet, but that doesn't mean it's any safer. Get a SEI/ASTM certified helmet and you are assured a certified protective

hard hat. The more expensive helmets will get you a prettier helmet overall, but it doesn't translate into more protection.

You only have one brain, and your skull can protect that brain only to a point. A horse's hoof, a rock, or even a branch can crack your skull and injure you for life. This one is essential; wear a hard hat.

This one is essential; wear a hard hat.

Some important facts regarding helmets:

- They "expire". Due to new technology, helmets are composed of foams, plastics, and other materials that can and do decompose over time, losing their integrity.

- The average lifespan of a helmet is about five years, but if you ride more often than 150 days a year, you may want to replace your helmet more often.

- Western style helmets are becoming all the rage now! These helmets are stunning in looks and most people won't realize that while you look stylish, you are also saving your noggin.

- The best and safest helmet for you is one that fits properly, is worn every time you ride and is replaced when it suffers any sort of blow, including your accidentally dropping it.

TIDBIT
Following all unplanned dismounts, even if the helmet looks fine, replace it with a new one.

93

THE *Myth*

To mount, lead your horse to a fence, rock, stump, or mounting block, and line him up so he is standing close enough for you to put your ankle over his back. Then, all you need to do is jump a little, and you're up and ready to ride.

Happily EVER AFTER

★ TIDBIT

Do not dismount at the mounting block. If your horse moves, or if you don't step down directly onto the block, you could fall onto the block and break your leg, arm, or back.

You are most vulnerable when you mount and dismount because you are neither mounted nor dismounted, and it's easy to lose your balance. It's crucial that you keep your horse under control while in such a precarious position.

Using a mounting block is best for your horse so that your weight doesn't pull him sideways as you struggle to get on. The extra height provided by the block causes less strain on his spine, shoulders, and hips, and is also better for you own spine, hips and knees as well.

Properly mount by leading your horse to a stable mounting block and lining him up so that the block is under the left stirrup. Be sure the block is not right under him so that when you are mounted and ready to go, he won't be forced to negotiate the obstacle.

Hold the reins in your left hand as you stand on the block. Ideally, you will be facing his tail, and your left rein will be a tad shorter than the right one. This way, if he walks or moves before you are ready, you can stop him from

> You are most vulnerable when you mount and dismount because you are neither mounted nor dismounted, and it's easy to lose your balance.

dragging you. By keeping your near rein shorter, if he moves, he can't move off in a straight line. Be careful not to pull that inside rein so tight that it causes him to swing his hindquarters away from you.

When mounting, put your left foot into the stirrup or iron and straighten that leg so that you are standing as you swing your right leg slowly over his back. Be careful not to inadvertently kick his rump as you do this, and then lower your bottom gently into the saddle as though you were a feather settling on a pond. Once you are seated, have your horse stand still for a moment until you give the cue to walk forward.

The best way to dismount is to lift your right leg over his rump so that you are standing on your left foot while leaning over with your tummy over horse's back. Then, kick your left foot out, then slide off. This method will keep you from being dragged should your horse move off while your foot is still in the stirrup.

THE *Myth*

When riding, shove your foot securely into the stirrup. Be sure your boot is in all the way to the heel so the stirrup will hold you on.

Happily EVER AFTER

TIDBIT
Stirrups in Western riding are the equivalent of Irons in English.

Stirrups (Western) and irons (English) are the part of the saddle that your foot rests on. Anyone ever riding bareback for more than an hour knows how your legs tire and your feet may swell, so having a place to set your feet helps prevent this from happening. The stirrups also allow you to hold your leg in the correct position for the discipline you are riding. Hunters and jumpers, for example use the irons to hold their leg and body in the jump or two-point position.

If you were to fall off your horse with your foot shoved through to the heel, you might not be able to get your foot loose before your upper body hits the ground, and you would be dragged by the horse. Needless to say, your bouncing body will scare him into running even faster. If the saddle ends up under the horse, even more entanglement of horse, saddle, and you happens. Best case, you have a broken leg and some bruises. No need to discuss the worst case.

Generally speaking, the stirrup is not a platform to stand on; nor is it meant to shove your foot into to secure you onto the horse.

The widest part of your foot should rest lightly on the base of the stirrup or iron with enough pressure to keep your lower leg still and quiet, but not so much as to make you stand. The ball of your foot should rest lightly on the base of the stirrup, allowing your ankle to flex.

Generally speaking, the stirrup is not a platform to stand on; nor is it meant to shove your foot into to secure you onto the horse.

When riding Western, cutting horse riders using the oxbow stirrup are the exception to this rule, and the arch of the foot rests on the bar. English riders can opt for safety irons that give way if the foot gets stuck.

THE *Myth*

Everyone knows how to get a horse to go; just lean forward and slam those heels into his sides. Stopping him is just as simple; throw your body back, shove your feet forward past his shoulder, and haul back on the reins.

Happily EVER AFTER

True horsemanship is not domination over the animal. Rather, it is the ability to communicate your desires to the horse in the subtlest way possible.

This simply translates to "less is more," and it means your goal should be to get the desired response from the horse without letting anyone see what you're doing. Imagine a dance couple on stage. The man guides the woman across the floor with barely a perceptible touch. This is what you strive for with your partner, the horse: invisible, quiet cues and commands that communicate what you want without the hoopla and shouting you observe in many beginners and some wannabe "trainers."

> Unless the horse is desensitized to the point of not caring, a kick to his sides could land you across the state line.

If your new trainer resorts to loud verbal reprimands, whips, or drugs, get a new one. Quiet body and mind connect better than shouting and jumping, which only add fear into the equation.

Horses are very sensitive and can feel the lightest fly or mosquito land on them. Imagine what a swift kick will do! Unless the horse is desensitized to the point of not caring, a kick to his sides could land you across the state line.

The cue to stop consists of more than just pulling back on the reins. The rest of your body must also give him that same command; your energy must lower, your upper torso must not lean forward, and your legs must not be squeezing or gripping his barrel.

Done properly, the cue to go forward is invisible and felt by the horse as soon as you bring your energy up while tensing your calves. Stopping him is equally quiet, and it is cued by the rider stopping the movement in her lower back and pelvis.

TIDBIT

The more violent and severe your aids, the more desensitized your horse will become over time.

THE *Myth*

The best way to stay on a horse is to wrap your ankles around the horse's barrel and grip hard. If you need to catch your balance, use your reins by sticking your elbows out to the sides and fly like a duck.

Happily EVER AFTER

Your inner thigh muscles are the ones you want to primarily use since calves and ankles aren't nearly as large or as strong. Ride in the same posture you walk— keep your feet under you, your elbows at your sides, and your head up.

Hanging on with your ankles gives the command to go faster, which would be the last thing you would want if you were off balance. The best way to stay on a horse is to keep your muscles relaxed and supple and your body centered.

It's quite simple, really; rather than squeezing your horse, let your legs hang as if they were wet towels. Grip with your thighs only if you feel you are losing your balance and may fall. Otherwise, just sit there.

Grip with your thighs only if you feel you are losing your balance and may fall.

★
TIDBIT
Riding a horse is like sitting in a canoe. Stay upright and keep your lower back supple; tense muscles will cause you to capsize.

Never use your reins for balance; it hurts your horse! Even though humans use shoulders and elbows for balance, while riding, this is not the case. Shift your center of balance down low, into your pelvis, and ride with light hands. Your elbows should never leave your sides and become wings; they should hang below your shoulders and help your hands deliver messages to your horse by opening and closing their angles.

THE *Myth*

Most beginners keep their toes pointed like a ballerina en pointe, and pull their heels up and back. This rider leans over the horse's withers, shoulders hunched, with her knees pulled up and her toes pointed to the ground. Usually, the horse will have a hollow back and a high head as he braces against this rider's hard hands and imbalance.

Happily EVER AFTER

Every single riding instructor you'll ever have will emphasize "heels down." However, the why of this set-in-eternity rule is often disregarded. With your heels down, you can better shift when your center of balance is downward, away from your chest and shoulders.

Heels down allows the rider to shift her weight back easier, use her knee and hip joints more effectively, and keep her balance better. Based on this, "heels down" is pretty much all you should need to know to be able to ride in a balanced manner, but we all know that's not the case.

In real life, your heels don't have to be down as much as you might think; just a tiny bit lower than the ball of your foot will allow your leg muscles and tendons to help you use your pelvis, hip, knee, and ankle joints to follow the movement of your horse more easily.

★
TIDBIT
If your knees or ankles hurt after riding, lengthen your stirrups and remember to let your legs hang long and relaxed.

Heels down too far can cause your feet to be too far forward and force you to use your hands to balance. Try to think of lengthening your legs and letting your heels drop rather than forcing them down and causing your legs to stiffen.

If the rider points the toes down, she will curl her body forward and raise her hands and her feet to try and stay on the horse. This "Humpty Dumpty" stance makes it difficult to stay on since once you are in the fetal position, your body resembles an egg, and, well, eggs roll.

Heels down helps lengthen your leg and keep your pelvis loose enough to follow your horse.

Heels down too far can cause your feet to be too far forward and force you to use your hands to balance.

THE *Myth*

Your saddle perpetually leans to one side. Obviously, something is wrong with your horse. No matter how tightly you cinch your horse, you find that you are always leaning to one side, or maybe it's your riding buddy who points out your listing ways. You can't really tell for sure if you're listing, and, really, what difference will it make anyway? You're used to it, and your horse doesn't seem to care, so you just keep riding. One day, you find yourself under the horse or on the ground.

Happily EVER AFTER

If you know you suffer from a crooked spine (scoliosis) or uneven hips, tilted pelvis, uneven femurs, or collapsed joints, it is simply a matter of being creative to fix the imbalance.

You may notice that you're not sitting centered and that your horse prefers going one direction more than another. Take a look at your balance and form, and be sure his preferring one direction over another isn't due to your constant imbalance and his desire to "fix" it by keeping himself under you.

If you continue riding off-center, the ride will happen where you are unable to stay on your horse since gravity will ultimately win. There are some things that could be causing you to not sit centered, such as a broken saddle tree, a loose girth, your horse suffering functional short limb disparity, scoliosis, your own uneven pelvis, or even a broken-down saddle pad. Once you have determined the problem, you can find a fix.

Here are some things to try:

- Examine your saddle from all angles and feel for any odd bulges or depressions underneath that may cause it to sit incorrectly.

- Check the girth, and be sure it is centered under the horse.

- Get a professional saddle fitter out to be sure your saddle fits both you and your horse.

- Ask someone to take your picture from the back and from the front as you ride, and then look at your own posture. (Don't forget to look at the level of your shoulders, elbows, hip bones, knees, and feet to be sure it's not you who is crooked.)

If you know you suffer from a crooked spine (scoliosis) or uneven hips, tilted pelvis, uneven femurs, or collapsed joints, it is simply a matter of being creative to fix the imbalance. Shimming your saddle pad may help level your hips or compensate for your horse's short limb disparity. Once you know you are truly sitting centered, balanced, and straight in the saddle, give yourself a little time to get used to the new feel. Spend a few rides just walking, and let your muscles relearn how they should respond.

It is not normal and okay to ride without a centered balance; it is detrimental to your horse's well-being and, ultimately, yours too.

TIDBIT
An off-center saddle indicates a problem, and a thorough examination of the horse, the rider, and the tack is a must.

Don't Trot.

THE *Myth*

Trotting is just too rough, so either walk or lope (canter) everywhere. If you do trot, be sure and do so by standing in the stirrups so the saddle doesn't slap your bottom.

TIDBIT
The secret to sitting the trot is to let your pelvis move independently from the rest of your body—just like doing a hula dance. (A nice vacation to Hawaii can be very helpful.)

Happily EVER AFTER

The trot is a diagonal, two-beat gait meaning that a horse trots in a similar manner to how we walk. Right front and left hind move simultaneously together, followed by the left front and right hind. The result is a forward-left-right movement much like when you jog on your own two legs.

When you stand up in the stirrups at the trot, unless you are competent at riding two-point (jump position), you are throwing your horse off balance, and yet you are expecting him to carry you in a safe manner. He needs his rider centered and stable on his back so he can move correctly and safely. Running everywhere is dangerous for horse and rider as well as others in your path.

Learn to sit the trot. Understand that it is a rough gait, and you will feel the jarring throughout your body—this feeling is normal. Watching your horse move can help you to visualize how you will need to move your hips and lower back.

The first step to sitting a trot is to become aware of how your own body moves while jogging without your horse. (Yes, you'll need to do this on your own—slowly

> You'll feel your hips move independently of your shoulders, hands, and feet.

around your living room is fine.) You'll feel your hips move independently of your shoulders, hands, and feet. In your pelvis, you'll notice a forward and sideways motion mixed with a little up and down movement. You should try tensing your back, your legs, and your shoulders; can you still jog easily? No, and that's exactly true when you're riding; keep every muscle soft and supple, and you'll be able to follow the movement instead of bouncing against it.

Once you understand these basics, try riding your horse, just walking at first, while letting him carry you. Close your eyes and feel the motion, stay soft and relaxed, and then bump him up into a slow jog and let your pelvis follow the motion. Remember to soften your lower back enough that your back pockets move left and then right, with the horse, and you will have the sitting trot down much more quickly than you'd ever imagined.

Strive for this simple accomplishment, and you will keep your horse happy and comfortable too. Besides, once you nail the sitting trot, learning to post and then canter is much easier.

THE *Myth*

While riding, if you are frightened or your horse is startled, scream loudly and continually for help. Clamp your legs tightly while digging your heels into his sides, and remember to lean forward so you are screaming directly into his ear. As the horse runs faster, yell louder for help and really hang on with your ankles.

★

TIDBIT
Think fast, move slowly,
and keep quiet.

Happily EVER AFTER

Remember that part about keeping your horse feeling safe? Screaming is pretty much a guaranteed prelude to disaster. Horses react by moving fast to sounds and to high-pitched, fear-laden screams in particular. This doesn't mean that you can't be afraid, but it does mean you must lock your full-throttled screams inside.

The secret to not screaming is to train yourself to be silent; no matter how frightened you are, or how badly you feel, the need to let out a banshee yelp must be stifled. You must keep your horse feeling safe. If you can think fast and say nothing, you'll be better able to help your horse calm down.

Easier said than done, right? One method to teach yourself to stay quiet while in a state of panic is to play a game with friends in which you'd normally scream out

Silence is your best friend when you are frightened.

in jubilation for winning, except, this time, instead of talking or whooping with joy, play in complete silence. Another way to practice controlling your emotions is to go to an amusement park and ride a roller coaster, but don't even whisper when all you really want to do is scream. By doing these things, you are teaching yourself to pay attention to your reactions and to temper your voice.

An even bigger advantage is the knowledge you'll gain to be able to control your emotional outbursts and subsequently keep your horse safe, which, of course, ultimately keeps you alive.

Silence is your best friend when you are frightened. Hold it together until after you leave your horse; then scream and shout all you want. Loud noises scare him, and you must always keep him feeling safe. Silence is golden, and it will also keep you alive.

THE *Myth*

Keep one hand on the saddle or hang on to the horn at all gaits. If you hang on with one hand at all times, you'll be safe.

Happily EVER AFTER

Hanging on tightly with one hand will not keep you on the horse. A death grip on the saddle horn, the pommel (front of the saddle), or even a panic strap makes your spine twist so that your body is out of alignment, thus throwing you off balance. Once you are out of balance, you are unable to use your own center of gravity to stay on the horse. Imagine a tightrope walker walking over the Grand Canyon with one shoulder leading the way; she's not likely to get far.

Here's the secret trick to riding a horse: Sit on him as though you are standing squarely on your own two feet and keep your left leg on the left side of

Remember to keep your lower leg relaxed and off of your horse.

the horse and your right leg on the right side of the horse. In all seriousness, this is how you should ride—as you would sit in a boat on a lake—balanced, soft, and centered. Your legs are stronger than your arms, so gripping with your inner thighs when you feel yourself slipping will keep you balanced and aboard.

If you feel you must hang on to stay on, ride while your horse is being lunged at a walk and drop your stirrups. Work up to riding with no hands to teach your body where "center" is and how to follow the movement with your hips and pelvis. Remember to keep your lower leg relaxed and off of your horse.

★

TIDBIT
An independent seat
and hands mean you
don't use your arms to
stay on the horse; that's
what your legs are for!

THE *Myth* **Natural aids and artificial aids are terms that mean nothing to you.**

Happily EVER AFTER

Natural aids are tools you always have with you because they are a natural part of you. Your voice, your legs, your hands, your seat, your demeanor, your humor, your posture, and your energy are all called "natural aids," and all are used to communicate with a horse.

Artificial aids are things that you must pick up or put on. Examples are whips, spurs, bridles, halters, ropes, and drugs of any variety. Artificial aids are anything you use to communicate with a horse that is not a part of your natural self.

Both natural and artificial aids are used every time we interact with a horse unless the animal is at liberty, wearing no tack, and you are not using a whip to make him go.

Traditionally, artificial aids reinforce natural aids and are used to discipline a horse.

Traditionally, artificial aids reinforce natural aids and are used to discipline a horse. It is important to understand that punishment or using artificial aids long-term is not a good way to train a horse or to communicate with him.

As always, it is your responsibility to keep your horse feeling safe at all times. Artificial aids intimidate and command through pain or fear, so use things that you must pick up or put on either him or you as little as possible. By communicating your wishes through kindness and compassion, you will reinforce your bond with your horse every time you work with him.

DEATH TIP
78

You've Got Spurs That Jingle, Jangle, Jingle, So Wear Them All The Time.

THE *Myth*

Wearing spurs is essential to being a good rider. Besides, spurs look cool and should be worn at all times.

Happily EVER AFTER

Spurs are an artificial aid that should be used by only the most experienced rider and, even then, as an aid, not as an everyday accessory.

Ideally, spurs are worn for only a few minutes to help the horse understand cues he may not be learning without them, or to reinforce or refine a cue at higher levels of riding. In the hands, or rather, on the feet, of beginners, spurs are the perfect storm brewing should the rider inadvertently poke the horse when all she meant to do was hang on with her ankles.

The reason spurs work and can be an important tool is that they allow the horse while under saddle to feel the same cue that he learned on the ground. Imagine teaching him to do a turn on the forehand from the ground—he is supposed to stand still on the front end and rotate his hindquarters around. You can touch his side and hold his head at the same time since you're beside him, but when you are riding, you can only touch his side with your calf or heel. If he doesn't understand what you want, and you apply a precisely focused pressure point, he will get the idea easily. However, a beginner or even an intermediate rider may inadvertently apply too much pressure, resulting in his feeling pain and leaping forward.

A rider who is unable to stay on without using her feet and ankles will actually be telling him to run fast. A train wreck is all one can expect in this scenario.

A well-trained horse, used to being ridden in spurs is oftentimes highly reactive to leg pressure, so beginners need to be aware of this heightened sensitivity when riding.

A horse can feel a gnat on his side, so imagine what the pressure of metal gouging or even just pressing on the skin must feel like to him. But in the right hands, or rather on experienced heels, spurs can be a helpful and useful training tool.

Leave the artificial aids such as spurs to the professionals until you are capable of controlling your leg movement and balance one hundred percent of the time. Spurs are fine as a fashion accessory, but if you don't have an independent seat and hands, take the spurs off before you saddle up.

The rounded portion of the spur is called the rowel. The jingle bobs are metal pieces that hang from the spur and make the sound we associate with walking while wearing spurs. Some horses hear the spurs jangling and know the rider is wearing them before the metal ever touches their sides.

A well-trained horse, used to being ridden in spurs is oftentimes highly reactive to leg pressure, so beginners need to be aware of this heightened sensitivity when riding.

THE *Myth*

Collection occurs when the horse's head is tucked, and his neck arches, and he prances along and looks beautiful. It's okay to use any gadget on him to get the results you want—his neck arched and his gait springy.

Happily EVER AFTER

Collecting your horse is something most riders strive for; it's the end-all regarding true riding, especially for dressage riders. Picture the Lipizzaner stallions of Vienna. Nothing prettier! But collection is not only about how a horse looks—it's not just his head carriage or his light, fancy footwork.

A truly collected horse is on the bit and uses his hindquarters as his "engine," though his front end is plenty engaged too. His back shortens, his front end lightens, and he moves fluidly, easily, and athletically. His back rises slightly when his hind end gets under him, and his head and neck balance him as he carries a rider with power and grace.

False collection occurs when a horse with an arched neck and a tucked chin holds his head perfectly steady, and, yet, he is not collected at all since his carriage is all wrong. When a horse is collected, he does much more with his entire mind and body than just flex at the poll.

Horses are more than the physical animal you see, and their emotional side is far more fragile than most people believe. Constricting a horse's movement is like a small

> When a horse is collected, he does much more with his entire mind and body than just flex at the poll.

death to him, yet many "trainers" and novices believe this is exactly how to get the horse to look animated, collected, and together.

Many people use gadgets to "teach" the horse how to move in this manner, thinking the horse is correctly collected, but, in reality, he is over bent in his poll, moving behind the bit and strung out behind. Tie-downs, martingales, draw reins, and side reins are artificial aids that can be helpful in training if used correctly and with consideration for the horse, but they can, like a whip, also destroy a horse's training experience.

When we crank a horse's head in to his chest using gear made for—what seems to be—exactly that purpose, we are eliminating his ability to move naturally. Get expert help in this area from someone who does more than just compress the horse from nose to heart girth.

Artificial aids can help achieve lightness and self-carriage, along with true collection, but used incorrectly, or too harshly, they can also destroy a horse's natural way of going. Consider the whole horse, not just his head and neck, when determining if he is collected or not.

TIDBIT
When teaching a horse to be collected, be sure you are correctly sitting centered so he may balance himself and carry you with ease.

THE *Myth*

If your horse won't cross the stream, whip him. Your horse won't go fast enough; whip him. Your horse won't load into a trailer; whip him.

Happily EVER AFTER

A whip, like any other artificial aid, can be a helpful tool if used properly or, if used improperly, it can become an implement resembling a weapon rather than a training tool.

A whip is not necessary every time you work your horse or encounter problems with him. If this particular artificial aid is used, remember that being hit hurts—not only physically, but emotionally too. Once hit, a horse will from then on react with a different light in his eyes. He may become completely pliable and obedient, or he may become resentful and stubborn. He may submit and obey your will, or he may fight your will with all he has.

Some people call whips by different names—cute terms that disguise their true intention—so know what tool you are using and why. Identifying a whip is easy; they are all fairly similar. Don't be fooled by sweet labels that falsely brand the truth.

A whip is not necessary every time you work your horse or encounter problems with him.

A whip can help guide a horse by presenting a visual cue and can also add the element of touch to signify what you want. An example of a whip used as an extension of your arm to help guide him might be applying the tip lightly to his rump to ask him to move away. In this case, a whip is beneficial to both horse and rider.

You can be clear of your own attitude by evaluating your expectations of the outcome you want. Expecting anything other than an "ah-ha moment" from your equine buddy is a red flag and signifies your need to walk away and come back when you've calmed down.

If your intention is to cause fear or pain, you have no right to approach any horse—especially while armed.

Use this particular weapon with the lightest touch and with no malice toward the horse.

DEATH TIP

81

Horses Like To Greet
Unknown Horses, So Let Them.

THE *Myth*

When out trail riding, allow your horse to say hello to all horses along the way. Horses want to greet one another, even if there is a fence between them, and if that fence is three-strand smooth wire, so what?

Happily EVER AFTER

There are many problems here—from contracting disease to potential injury to your own horse, the other horse, or even you. Horses touching noses transmit many diseases, and you just don't know if the one you're allowing your horse to touch is healthy or not.

Often upon meeting, horses will squeal, snort, and strike out with a front leg before turning around and kicking out with both hinds. Most often, stallions and mares do this, but geldings also exhibit this behavior.

Since you can't know if the horse on the other side of the fence is healthy, or if he will strike, you also don't know if it will bite or kick. Any of these actions can cause your own horse to reciprocate with the same action. There are many possible train wrecks here, but the worst could include horses with broken legs, your own broken leg, a horse impaled on a fence post after rearing, or a broken fence and loose horses.

TIDBIT

When horses first meet, they often run together before stopping to sniff each other and be in one another's body space.

The easiest way to avoid any of these scenarios is to keep a full horse-length away from any other horse at all times. Give a wide berth to horses on the other side of a fence, even if you know them and think it's safe.

Often upon meeting, horses will squeal, snort, and strike out with a front leg before turning around and kicking out with both hinds.

From a safe distance, watch the horse(s) on the other side of the fence and wait for them and for your own horse to settle before commencing on with your ride. A high head, snorting, raised tail, running a fence line...these are all signs that all involved are too excited and a moment is needed to calm down before continuing on.

THE *Myth*

Whatever is wrong with your horse when you ride; fix the problem with a better, bigger, harder, or different type of bit. Bits fix everything.

Happily EVER AFTER

Each rider must have control of her horse, and a horse's mouth is sensitive, so it makes sense that most people subscribe to using bits as the best means to the end. Choosing the right bit can be a daunting task, and the more you read, the more confused you may become.

The bigger-hammer theory is not a good one to apply when trying to gain control of your horse. Go back to basics if you are having trouble, and hire a professional trainer to help fix any problems before they get worse.

When choosing a bit for your horse, the "less is more" rule applies. English or Western, these are the simplest guidelines to follow: Thicker mouthpieces are less harsh than thin ones. Short shanks have less leverage than long ones. Copper mouthpieces cause a metallic reaction that some horses don't like. High

ports (the center rounded portion of a Western bit's mouthpiece) jab into the horse's palate.

Horses move away from pressure, and more pressure on the mouth can cause rearing, reckless backing, and sudden stops. Until your hands and seat are independent, do not ride using a bit—especially a harsh one.

Horses have different depth palates—some are low, and some are high. The tongue thickness of each horse is different as well. Knowing the anatomy of your horse's mouth will help you choose the correct bit for him. To determine your horse's palate, gently insert your fingers in the side of his mouth and feel the space between his tongue and palate. If it is low, you may want to consider a bit with two breaks in the mouthpiece.

> ♘
> **Knowing the anatomy of your horse's mouth will help you choose the correct bit for him.**

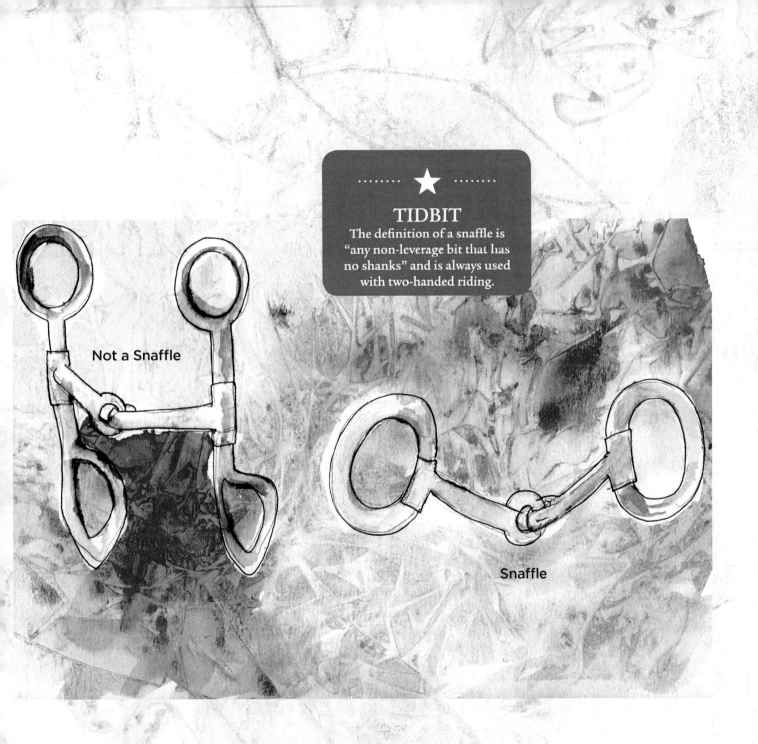

Not a Snaffle

Snaffle

THE *Myth*

In your opinion, flash, figure-eight, and drop nosebands are the best inventions since the wheel. They look pretty cool, and they have the added bonus of keeping your horse's mouth shut.

Happily EVER AFTER

TIDBIT
Nosebands of any kind can cause distress and inhibit your horse's breathing if cinched down too tightly.

If he's in a snaffle, be sure there are no wrinkles at the corners of his lips.

You want your horse to trust you, to feel safe with you, and to want to work for you, giving his best. Tying his mouth shut is counterproductive to each of these desired outcomes. You may have assumed his gnashing teeth, open mouth, and tongue gymnastics were due to his purposeful misbehaving. Before jumping to conclusions, first check his teeth. Is he in any discomfort or pain? If he's under the age of five, are his adult teeth erupting?

If your horse has an overactive mouth, it may be that he never learned his responsibility in carrying the bit himself so his mouth stays quiet and he understands what is expected from him. Many trainers start a young horse in a snaffle bridle, but they tighten the headstall too short. They may believe they are doing the right thing by creating two or three wrinkles at the corners of the mouth, but this is completely incorrect

If he's in a snaffle, be sure there are no wrinkles at the corners of his lips. Don't forget to pull that noseband off and replace it with a simple cavesson that is properly adjusted and not too tight. It may take him a week or so to forget his open-mouthed ways—and trust you and your hands—but you will see improvement. Be sure your hands are steady and soft, and don't pull on his mouth. Remember, you are building trust here! Be sure your horse's open mouth isn't due to your hard hands, ill-fitting tack, or his discomfort.

THE *Myth*

On the trail or in the ring, remember it is each person for himself or herself. You are not responsible for anyone else. If riding in the ring, play music loudly, let your horse get too close to others, or, even better, run madly about, and change directions often. If you have a dog, be sure and let him run loose in the arena too.

If riding on the trail, just ride and don't worry about anyone else. If you encounter low branches, hold onto them as you pass, then let them loose so they fly back to hit the person behind you in the face.

Happily EVER AFTER

On the trail, it is easy to forget about the person behind you, but it's important to help others have a good ride too. If you must touch a low-hanging branch, warn your riding buddy, so she has time to stop before it slaps her or her horse in the face.

If you must suddenly stop, signal the person behind you by putting your hand down, palm facing backward, and say, "Stopping." Be courteous and point out potential dangers such as holes, wire, branches, bad footing, or anything else that may cause others harm.

In the arena, be aware of others, and ride with consideration for them. Go the same way as the crowd, and ask if you may reverse before doing so. When passing, offer the term "rail" if you're going to track near the wall, and use "inside" if tracking nearer the center. If someone is having a problem in the arena, stop your horse so theirs may settle. When obstacle training, be aware of others in the area in case your horse spooks and theirs follow suit.

Help others by being a conscientious and considerate rider. It's free!

If you have a dog, leave him at home. If your barn allows dogs on the premises, follow the barn's set of rules. If no rules are posted, ask the manager, ask the other riders, or leave Fido in the car with windows down so he doesn't overheat.

Your responsibility as a horse owner-rider-handler is to be aware of your surroundings, the people and animals, and respect what others are doing. Help others by being a conscientious and considerate rider. It's free!

★

TIDBIT
People won't want to ride with you if you are inconsiderate.

DEATH TIP 85

Sit Back, Relax, And Enjoy The Ride.

THE *Myth*

You've had a hard day; it's time to relax and let the horse do the work. Any of the following examples are applicable:

- You're tired and just feel like zoning out while your horse carries you through the woods.

- You haven't seen your friends since last weekend and want to catch up while riding.

- Your cell phone rings and you really need to get it. One short text won't hurt.

Happily EVER AFTER

Talking on your cell phone, texting, or laughing with friends are all great ways to guarantee you aren't paying attention to what your horse is thinking or how he may react if anything unexpected happens. It will be unexpected only because you chose not to be present and aware of his emotional state and needs.

Every moment with a horse is a silent conversation, and the horse's body language is how he communicates what he is feeling and what he might do. If you are paying attention, the conversation is never-ending and keeps you constantly aware of one another.

Most people ride because they want the resulting connection and relationship. These just improve when you focus on your horse first. Staying present, aware, and in tune with your horse keeps you connected and lets you know his emotional state and ultimately keeps you both safe.

> Every moment with a horse is a silent conversation, and the horse's body language is how he communicates what he is feeling and what he might do.

TIDBIT
If you are preoccupied, you might want to use your distracted energy cleaning tack instead of riding.

DEATH TIP 86

Double Your Fun.

THE *Myth*

Ride double with your best friend, bareback, at a gallop. Yee-haw!

Happily EVER AFTER

Do not do this. Just don't.

It's self-explanatory, really. To start with, the two of you weigh too much for your horse's spine unless each rider weighs less than sixty pounds. Too much weight set on a horse's back over his lumbar region of his back can cause discomfort and damage.

A huge consideration is the fact that the second rider's legs will hang near the flank and this area is especially sensitive and ticklish for many horses. The sensation of heels digging into this part of his body may cause a normally calm and well-behaved horse to buck.

Since the two riders will move differently according to where they are perched on the horse, they may inadvertently give him conflicting signals. If he gets too worried, his answer may be to buck or bolt.

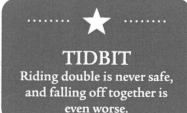

Too much weight set on a horse's back over his lumbar region of his back can cause discomfort and damage.

Increasing speed while riding double oftentimes causes an otherwise quiet horse to buck since the second rider can't grip without using her feet and ankles. Both riders will bounce more with speed and each will struggle to stay on. Galloping while riding double is a good way to lose your balance and fall off— that's especially true for the person riding behind since the barrel of the horse is so wide that it's hard to stay balanced. When she goes off, she'll most likely pull the front rider off with her. Landings are harder on the person riding behind too; she gets to land on the ground first and then is smashed by her riding buddy, who crushes her. This second rider, who got landed on by the first, could suffer serious injuries. To top it all off, either rider could get kicked as the horse runs off into the sunset.

THE *Myth*

The horse in front of you is too slow, so letting yours tailgate may make him move faster. Be sure and let your horse put his nose, mouth, or chin on the other horse or let him nip his rump.

> ⭐
> ### TIDBIT
> While riding, your knee is at about the perfect height for a kicking horse's hoof to connect with if you are tailgating.

Happily EVER AFTER

No one likes being crowded, and horses are no different. Even horses that don't normally kick will let loose with both barrels if crowded.

Better to have your horse walk more slowly, or talk to your riding buddy and ask her either to speed up a bit or let you go first. Tailgating is dangerous for the lead horse if his heels get stepped on by your horse. And it's dangerous to your horse (and you!) if you allow this behavior. Even good equine friends will kick when another horse gets too close. Worst case, you get kicked, or you end up with a horse needing to be euthanized due to a broken leg.

Stay back at least one full horse length at all times and ask other riders to do the same. This amount of space allows time for the riders to react in case of an emergency too. If your group goes faster than a walk, increase the distance even more so that each horse has enough space to maneuver and riders have a chance to avoid each other.

To keep your horse from crowding, give him a task to complete to focus his attention in a good way to help him see you as his strong and capable leader.

Stay back at least one full horse length at all times and ask other riders to do the same.

THE *Myth*

You notice a horse with a red ribbon in his tail. Quick, run up behind him, and tell the owner how pretty it is.

Happily EVER AFTER

A red ribbon is a universal signal that the horse wearing it kicks, so beware of getting too close. Running or even walking up behind this horse will likely result in you being kicked.

If you see a horse with a red ribbon in his tail while riding on the trail or in the arena, be sure and stay back an extra few feet than you normally would. If passing that horse going the opposite direction, you won't see the ribbon in the tail, but the rider will warn you that he kicks. While trail riding, if you encounter a kicker, stop and ask the other rider what she'd like you to do get past. Sometimes, it's better to get off the trail and stand facing her as she passes, and other times, she'll ask you to pass while she stands still.

Tell your non-horsey friends what a red ribbon in the tail means, too. Some horses kick only other horses, but others will also kick at people.

Do not approach (especially from the rear) any horse with a red ribbon in his tail; that ribbon is not for looks. With that in mind, don't put a red ribbon in your own horse's tail unless he kicks other horses. The red ribbon is to be respected!

Do not approach (especially from the rear) any horse with a red ribbon in his tail; that ribbon is not for looks.

THE *Myth*

At the end of each and every ride, turn toward home at the exact same place on the trail, or, if in the arena, just gallop to the gate. Be sure to lean forward, kick hard, and yell loudly.

Happily EVER AFTER

One day you're out on a nice trail ride with friends. You reach your usual turnaround point with no intention of going home, but your horse doesn't know this. You aren't paying attention, and, suddenly, he's spun a U-turn so fast you find yourself on the ground wondering what happened.

Or, you stay on, the horse takes off at a full gallop, and you realize you have no brakes. Your friend's horse follows suit, and she screams loudly, inadvertently causing the horses to run even faster. You both make it back to the barn, where both horses slam on their newfound brakes at the fence, and you and/or your friend are catapulted headfirst into space.

This is how to train your horse to be "barn sour" and teach him to become dangerous and uncontrollable too.

This is how to train your horse to be "barn sour" and teach him to become dangerous and uncontrollable too.

Horses learn through repetition, context, and reward. While on the trail, or in the arena, if you dash for home at the end of your ride, you are teaching the horse this event happens when your time together is over. He will anticipate the ending of your ride and may conclude that running to the barn will end the ride, and he can get back to eating or hanging out with his horse friends.

Always walk the entire way toward home once you are within two miles of the barn. This rule helps your horse keep a calm demeanor, gives him time to cool down so you don't have to hand walk once back at the barn, and allows you to end the ride happily and safely.

DEATH TIP
90
▾

Trail Ride Alone. Tell No One.

THE *Myth*

You want to ride, and there is no one to go with you. No need to tell anyone and no need to take a cell phone or tell anyone where you are going. You've done this a thousand times before, and nothing bad has ever happened. You tack up and head out on your own with thoughts of a pleasant ride dancing in your head.

Happily EVER AFTER

What you least expect to happen does, and your horse spooks at a bird taking flight, then stumbles and falls. He's completely lame and bleeding, and once you pick yourself up off the ground, you realize your own leg won't support your weight. Alone, with a lame horse and unable to walk on your own, you can just call for help. Only you didn't bring your phone. Surely, someone will come find you; except no one knows where you are.

Horses spook at smaller things more often when alone because they look to their herd members for safety. Especially on windy days or when storms are predicted, try to ride in company since these conditions make most horses edgy and hyper alert.

If you do choose to ride solo, be on alert for his constant wariness, and ride with caution. Try to stay close to the barn so search teams can find you more easily if needed. Take your phone with you. Most times, with even minimal cell

When trail riding, always carry your cell phone, a first aid kit for you and your horse, a hoof pick, and a pocketknife.

★ TIDBIT
If your horse is afraid of sounds, a string of beads and tiny bells hung around his neck makes a soothing rhythmic sound as the horse moves.

service, you can at least text if a call won't go through, and your GPS can guide rescue teams to you in the event of an emergency. Be sure and tell someone where you are going and when you intend to return. Ask that person to check on you if you haven't reported back in a reasonable amount of time.

Riding with others is safer than riding alone, but if you are solo, take precautions and keep safety in mind. When trail riding, always carry your cell phone, a first aid kit for you and your horse, a hoof pick, and a pocketknife.

THE *Myth*

When trail riding, you need to be prepared for anything so bring along as much as you are able to carry.

Happily EVER AFTER

A rider that well prepared would absolutely have the best chance of surviving pretty much any disaster. The thing is, most riders are on the trail for an average of two hours each ride. Most carry the essentials; a hoof pick, a small first aid kit that can be used for horse or rider, their phone with GPS system, a trail map if in new territory, and many ride with a halter and lead on their horse. A roll of heavy duty tape is not a bad thing to add to your arsenal of things to take on each ride in case a shoe is thrown and the horse needs a temporary fix to get back to the trail head. Each item brought on a trail ride can make any potentially disastrous event easier to deal with, but too many items can also add to the potential disaster count.

No matter what you choose to carry along, be

Tie everything down tightly and securely so nothing falls and spooks the other horses with you.

sure to desensitize your horse to each item and warn your riding buddies of anything that may scare their horses so they too, can be prepared. For example, if you like to bring a bedroll, teach your horse that if it comes untied and drapes over his haunches, it won't kill him. If you carry items that jingle and make odd noises, be sure he knows about those as well and isn't afraid of them.

Tie everything down tightly and securely so nothing falls and spooks the other horses with you. Tuck your shirt into your pants and you may avoid getting it caught over the saddle horn while riding western. Wear a belt in case a rein breaks. Carry a pocket knife. Be certain you don't over-burden your horse weight wise by making him carry too much tack or too many things in your saddle bag.

A two hour trail ride probably won't warrant the need of a tent and bedroll, but a hoof pick, first aid kit and water are not bad choices.

THE *Myth*

A rearing horse is pretty and showing everyone how well you can ride is a bonus! While mounted, cue your horse to back up by yanking hard on the reins. Lean back and pull harder if he doesn't respond. Grit your teeth and grimace. Cuss, kick your feet forward, and set your shoulders. Yell at him. If the horse raises his head, pull back harder, and really get after him. He will likely rear, even if just an inch off the ground.

Once the adrenaline stops pumping through your body, realize how fun it was, and do it again. Soon, you will have a very dangerous animal that can't safely be ridden. Sell him, or give him away since he is no good, and remember there's no need to tell the buyer that he rears.

Happily EVER AFTER

There is absolutely no time that your horse's front feet should ever leave the ground together. Since horses move away from pressure, they will look for a way out of the uncomfortable situation you've created, so if you think about it, you've actually asked him to rear, not back up.

To properly back a horse up, first stop him squarely so that all four feet are under him. Sit quietly in the saddle, and take the slack out of the reins—don't pull!—while squeezing your knees together. Give the command that your horse move his feet by clucking to him or by lightly touching him with your calves. At the same time, picture that you are creating a wall in front of his nose, and ask him to move. Since he cannot go forward, he will look for another way to get away from the pressure.

The horse's head should dip toward the ground, and his weight should shift to his rear before he steps. A person

> Never yank the reins; they connect to his sensitive mouth, and the hard pulling will hurt him.

on the ground cueing for the backup helps the horse understand that these new signals mean he should step back. The second you feel your horse even think about shifting back onto his haunches, release the reins. When he actually does step, loosen them immediately, and praise with enthusiasm.

Never yank the reins; they connect to his sensitive mouth, and the hard pulling will hurt him. Never pull back until he rears; it's dangerous. If the horse loses his balance and he falls backward onto you, your own death may result.

Practice this exercise until all you need to do to get him stepping backward is to squeeze your knees while simultaneously sitting back lightly on your seat bones. Do this exercise in ultraslow motion, one step at a time, with reward (loosened reins and praise) at each step.

Cue with the lightest amount of pressure possible, and repeat often enough that as soon as you shift your weight, he steps backward. Aim for straight, slow, and attentive steps from him.

127

THE *Myth*

You've been riding all your life. You stay on, you go fast, and you know all you need to know. Your horse is at the trainer's only because he doesn't know anything.

Happily EVER AFTER

None of us rides exactly the same, and each person puts her own spin on the basics. For example, we all sit differently and use our natural aids with differing amounts of pressure. If your horse is with a trainer, it's a good assumption that the trainer rides by doing less and getting more out of each cue. Learning how to talk to your horse in a whisper with the touch of a feather is something to strive for.

Riding lessons taken from a qualified instructor are simply coaching sessions to help you better balance and interact with your horse. By letting an instructor watch you and give feedback, that instructor becomes like a talking mirror and can encourage the good stuff you already practice while curbing the bad.

Working with a trainer and taking lessons help the trainer to know how best to train your horse using methods tailored for you. The trainer can work him to better suit your natural abilities and can help adjust your way of riding so that you become a more efficient rider. Think of riding lessons in the same vein as learning to dance. Your partner is your horse, and when you each speak the same language and hear the same beat, the result is fluid and easy.

When your horse is in training, he learns everything through the person you pay to teach him, and you need to know the same things he learns. This doesn't mean your horse is stupid or that you can't ride; it means that you are taking lessons to help clarify the communication between your horse and you, and you both need to know what the trainer is teaching. Riding lessons are essential to bridging the gulf between you and your horse by teaching you and him the same language so that you can communicate clearly.

> **Learning how to talk to your horse in a whisper with the touch of a feather is something to strive for.**

DEATH TIP
94
▾

Problem Horses Need To Go.

THE *Myth*

Sell any horse you can't handle, but don't tell the buyer of any issues he may have while under saddle or in hand. You bought the horse, and the seller told you that he was a safe and reliable mount for a beginner, but you don't feel safe on him; he bucks and runs back to the barn, and when you feed him, he bites you. No one wants to buy a problem horse, so when you sell him because he's too much for you to handle, don't divulge this fact; just say you don't have time for him anymore.

Happily EVER AFTER

Aside from being unethical and dishonest, you are opening yourself up to a potential lawsuit if a buyer is hurt while trying out your bucking, bolting, biting horse.

The best way to sell a horse—or anything else for that matter—is to reveal all you know about him so a prospective buyer is aware of what problems the animal may have. If you don't, and the buyer gets hurt, you could be held liable. As a seller, you are responsible for representing the product (the horse) as honestly as you can.

Selling a horse can be frustrating and sometimes you may feel like throwing your hands in the air and giving up, but lying or omitting is not the best short cut to take. If you can't sell him on your own, hire a broker or a trainer to help you. Best scenario is to fix the problems before selling by getting him trained. It will cost you a bit up front, but you'll get more money for him potentially and even better, you won't lie awake at night wondering if the new owner is still alive.

As a seller, you are responsible for representing the product (the horse) as honestly as you can.

TIDBIT
Be the seller you want to buy from.

DEATH TIP
95

▼

Teach Your Horse To Spook.

THE *Myth*

Whenever you feel, see, or suspect your horse is scared, slow him down or stop. Be sure to pat and rub him, and in a high-pitched baby-talking voice, say, "It's okay, honey. Don't worry. Good boy!" If possible, be sure to turn his back to the scary object, and then trot briskly away.

Happily EVER AFTER

Praising in a high-pitched voice will indeed create a jumpy horse. This doesn't mean he's truly a spooky horse. He's just learned to jump, spook, and start so that you will comfort and praise him.

None of us can be taught to fear nothing, but you can help him overcome his fears by teaching him to control his emotions. Encourage him to be curious instead of fearful by encouraging and rewarding him when he is solid and steady instead of jittery and snorty.

Remember to keep your horse safe, and you will instinctively know to keep your focus simultaneously on him and your surroundings. You shouldn't look for things that will scare him; that's as bad as praising him for shying. But you need to be aware of how he sees the world.

Visit new places with a seasoned horse buddy, and stay calm and encouraging as he explores. Then go to less-stressful environments, and help him see that you are just as reliable as his horse friend at keeping him safe.

> Encourage him to be curious instead of fearful by encouraging and rewarding him when he is solid and steady instead of jittery and snorty.

The easiest and fastest way to stop a horse from spooking is to practice your leadership skills and to gain the trust of your horse. Spooked horses need to move their feet, so asking him to stand is not always a good solution. Better to move his feet in a specific pattern—have him do serpentines past the scary thing, and once he calms, work him in that area over and over if possible so that he learns there is nothing to fear, and you are a reliable leader. Never turn his back to the questionable place; he's a prey animal, and his instinct to run may take over.

Once a horse is able to control his own emotions and to trust that you will keep him safe, he becomes less fearful. Scary times demand a solid leader and some small tasks for your horse to perform. Circling him should never be a part of this repertoire because for half of the circle he will face the scary thing, but for the other half he will have his back to that scary thing.

★

TIDBIT
If your horse suddenly stops, raises his head, perks his ears, and snorts, let him look until he dips his nose a fraction of an inch before giving him a task to perform.

THE *Myth*

You feel like you're on a wagon that has three round wheels and one square one. "Hmmm. This is strange," you think, and then you happily continue on your ride.

Happily EVER AFTER

If you feel your horse moving in an odd, stilted manner, dismount and watch him walk so you can see which leg is affected. If you can't tell, try walking next to him, matching your stride exactly with his to see if there is a weird rhythm that indicates which foot he is favoring. Be sure to check that leg for any heat or swelling, cuts or abrasions. Pick the hooves, checking for stones, nails, or anything that shouldn't be there.

If you still can't tell, ask someone else to take a look, so when you call the veterinarian (and you should do this if in doubt of the severity of the issue), you'll be able to pass along key details about what is going on, such as whether there is any swelling, heat, cuts, etc.

If an experienced person can't determine the problem, call the vet. As strange as it seems, sometimes a horse

As strange as it seems, sometimes a horse with mouth or tooth issues will act lame.

with mouth or tooth issues will act lame. If your horse is on medication to help ease any kind of soreness or pain (navicular disease, coffin bone fracture, and hoof, back, or mouth problems) and he acts up or seems lame, remember that he may still be hurting and may need some downtime.

Riding an already lame horse could cause serious health problems for either of you, since horses in pain often decide the reason for their discomfort is you, the rider, and that the best way to lose the pain is to lose you. Before this happens, get off, check him for injury, and call your veterinarian.

A horse in pain is not predictable and is no longer safe to ride.

THE *Myth*

You can't ride your horse—that's why you're selling him—so make the buyer ride him first. Best scenario: The buyer doesn't bring a trainer along, and this is a first-time buyer and doesn't know any better.

★

TIDBIT
Well-behaved horses sell for more money. Pay a trainer to tune him up so he shows well.

Happily EVER AFTER

By making the buyer ride your horse first, you are putting that buyer in danger if you already know your horse is one to buck or bolt or rear. If the person gets hurt, he or she may sue you and win, but, even worse, you will know that you are responsible for another's pain. You will wonder if you should have warned the buyer ahead of time, and then you concoct some story about why the buyer should have known better.

It is never OK to put another person in harm's way. If you are afraid to ride your horse and have decided to sell him, tell all buyers every single undesirable thing your horse does and ask the buyer to bring a qualified trainer along. Sure, you won't be able to get as much for him, but you will sleep better and bask in the knowledge that you did the right thing.

You, the seller, should be able to demonstrate the horse while working with him on the ground and in the saddle, but if you can't, then hire a professional to help

If you can't handle your horse, don't expect someone else to be able to without getting hurt.

you. The trainer may take the horse into a short training tune-up session (a week or two) before actively marketing him. You will pay a commission, but the headache of doing it yourself is eliminated. The money spent to get your horse to a place where he is not dangerous may be recouped in the sale. Plus, if you decide to get another horse, have this same trainer help you become a better equestrian and have the trainer find your next mount for you.

If you can't handle your horse, don't expect someone else to be able to without getting hurt. Dangerous horses that inspire fear are made that way by humans; find a pro to help him get better before dumping him onto an unsuspecting stranger.

While Trail Riding In Hunting Areas, Walk Quietly And Wear Camo.

THE *Myth*

During hunting season, ride the trail in stealth mode so you don't bother the hunters or scare the game. Wear your best camouflage outfit. You'll blend right in and everyone will be happier.

Happily EVER AFTER

Hunters shouldn't shoot blindly, but sometimes, in thick brush or heavily treed areas, your horse may be mistaken for an elk or deer. Be sure you and your horse are highly visible, and make noise while riding in remote areas during hunting season. Wear bright orange clothing, and decorate your horse with orange flagging, saddle pad, and bridle. Add some bells to be as loud and as visible as possible. If riding with a friend— you should be—talk a lot and loudly so hunters know you are not game.

Hunting season coincides with the time frame when bears are intent on eating enough to survive winter hibernation, so tying bells onto your horse will also alert them and the hunters that you're near.

Train your horse to the sound of gunfire at home by desensitizing him using a cap pistol. If you don't know how to do this, hire a trainer.

Non-hunters, plan your pleasure trail ride for midday, as most hunters prefer to hunt in the early morning and late afternoon and evening.

Ride the area some time before hunting season starts, so you know where the hunters will likely be located. If you encounter hunters, be courteous, and let them know your planned route.

If you are a hunter hunting with a horse, you have other considerations—like training your horse to do things he normally wouldn't consider. Besides not fearing gunshots, he should be taught to tolerate the smell of blood and dead animals, ground-tie, and, should either be trained to hobbles or a highline.

It is imperative to know the horse you are hunting from so you know what to expect from each other.

Be sure you and your horse are highly visible, and make noise while riding in remote areas during hunting season.

THE *Myth*

The need for speed races through your veins. You believe the most fun thing to do while riding is to open your horse up and run full out. Wind in your hair, tears rolling down your cheeks, and his hooves pounding the ground in a blur. It's an open field; run!

Happily EVER AFTER

Riding fast is fun unless your horse falls, trips, hits hidden obstacles, breaks his leg by stepping into a hole, or gets so excited you are unable to stop him. Pick your galloping area carefully, and avoid places that are rocky, paved, overgrown with grass, or where gophers may have dug holes. You and your horse need to see what he is running over and through, so if there is tall grass or bushes, be careful to keep your speed down.

If you are riding in company, ask all riders if they are okay running, because not everyone has the experience to stay on. Hitting the ground at a full gallop hurts.

Remember that horses will become excited to run if you always hit Mach 9 at the same place on your rides. That excitement does not mean he "likes" to run; it means he knows what's

TIDBIT
A horse with a "blown mind" is one that usually has been run fast every ride. These ruined horses are hard to retrain and dangerous; you do want to avoid this.

> That excitement does not mean he "likes" to run; it means he knows what's coming.

coming. You are training him to respond in a specific manner when you are in a certain place. If galloping is part of your riding, vary the places, and on some rides, don't go faster than a walk. This helps him keep his sanity as well as keeping you in control.

Do not run through open fields or anywhere you can't see holes, wire, or other objects. You are obligated to keep your horse safe! What is perfectly safe to do at a walk may be quite dangerous at speed.

DEATH TIP 100

Tighten Your Cinch And Forget About It.

THE *Myth*

Once the cinch or girth is tightened, you're good to go for the entire ride. No need to check it before mounting or during your ride. You did it right the first time.

★ TIDBIT

Stretching your horse's front legs forward before mounting helps keep the skin beneath the cinch or girth from bunching up and rubbing to form a sore, called a 'gall'.

Happily EVER AFTER

If you tighten your cinch or girth when you saddle and then don't check it before mounting, you may find yourself under your horse, instead of on him. If you don't periodically check it to be sure it's still tight, it may loosen.

Even a tightened cinch or girth can allow the saddle—English or Western—to slip and slide on the horse's back, so the rider must constantly adjust the saddle to keep it centered. Look at your horse's mane and line the horn or the center of the pommel with it. Stand on one stirrup and bounce to shift the saddle back to center if needed.

An over-tight cinch or girth can make it hard for your horse to breathe and if he's uncomfortable enough, may cause him to buck, rear or balk, so if he begins acting differently, check your tack fit and cinch or girth before punishing him.

A properly adjusted cinch or girth is one that allows the saddle to sit comfortably. Pull it tight, but not with all your might.

Some horses will "blow up" until the cinch is tightened, then will relax so the saddle fits looser. They don't like to be squeezed!

A properly adjusted cinch or girth is one that allows the saddle to sit comfortably. Pull it tight, but not with all your might.

DEATH TIP
101

Horses Always Have
The Right Of Way.

THE *Myth*

You are on a horse, so you have the right of way. All people, including bicyclists and those driving vehicles, must yield to you, so you can ride in the middle of the road and cause traffic to stop.

Happily EVER AFTER

Your responsibility as an equestrian is to be observant while riding alongside a road. Acknowledge considerate drivers with a quick wave or a nod. Otherwise, both hands should be kept on the reins, except when signaling changes of direction. Yes, if you are on a horse on a road, you must signal your intent to turn or stop.

You should always wear fluorescent and reflective gear when riding on roads, whether the weather is good or bad and whether it is a bright sunny day or a dusky evening—which you should avoid anyway. Never take for granted that the driver of an approaching vehicle will see your horse or you.

Horses need to learn about traffic, and the best way to do this is to have an experienced and qualified trainer work with your horse so he understands how to behave.

Even the most sensible horse can get frightened and spin, or rear or bolt into traffic. Be safe, and get off if you must. Be aware, and be safe.

Tell your non-equestrian friends to slow down and stay at least twelve feet from the horse while driving past a rider. Who knows how many lives will be saved!

> Tell your non-equestrian friends to slow down and stay at least twelve feet from the horse while driving past a rider.

TIDBIT

Hand signals are as follows: Left hand up to turn right, outstretched to turn left, and hand pointing down to stop.

DON'T WORRY: BE HAPPY!

THE *Myth*

After reading 101 things that you must know, learn, and remember, you think it's too difficult and maybe you should just forget about being an equestrian. Yet you feel as if that proverbial "horse bug" has bitten, and you just have to plow forward.

Happily EVER AFTER

★

TIDBIT
A rider who understands how her horse thinks allows communication lines to be wide open, encouraging a true working relationship.

There are plenty more than 101 things to think about, practice, and do when with a horse; this is true. But you'll find that in a short amount of time, most of them become second nature.

The most important are as follows:

- Keep your horse feeling safe.
- Be confident, quiet, and aware.
- Plan ahead for any contingency by thinking "prevention."
- Hire a trainer and follow the trainer's advice.
- Listen to your horse, your instincts, and your instructor.
- Love your horse and have fun, and always be safe.

There are plenty more than 101 things to think about, practice, and do when with a horse; this is true.

Happy Trails!

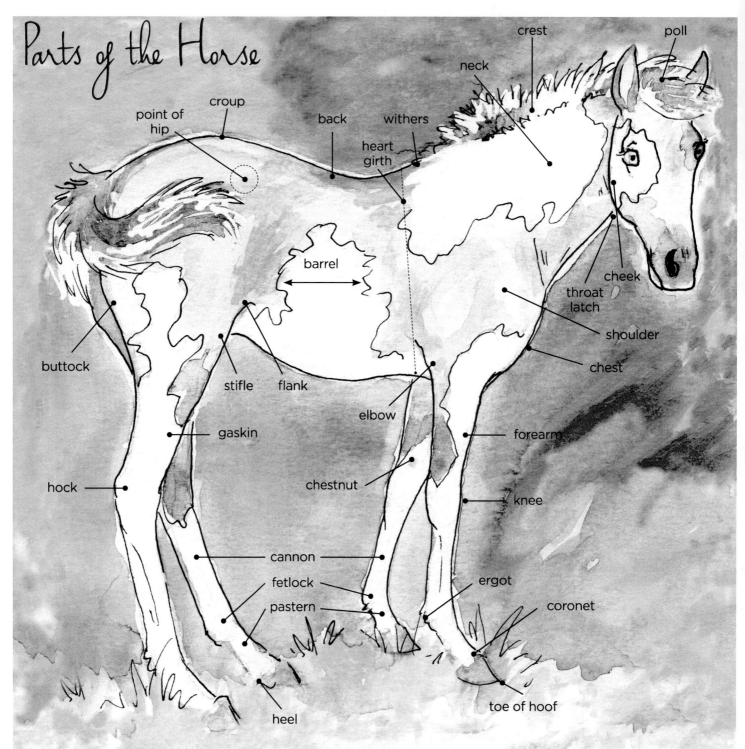

Parts of the Horse

crest

poll

neck

point of hip

croup

back

withers

heart girth

cheek

throat latch

shoulder

chest

barrel

buttock

stifle

flank

elbow

forearm

gaskin

chestnut

hock

knee

cannon

fetlock

ergot

pastern

coronet

heel

toe of hoof

GLOSSARY

AIDS: Signals from rider to horse using hands, legs, seat, weight, and voice to influence him are natural aids. Artificial aids are man-made devices such as a whip and spurs and may be used to reinforce the natural aids.

BARN SOUR: Also known as horse being herd bound and reluctant to leave other horses or the stable.

BIT: Traditionally the metal portion of a bridle, but may be made of plastic, rope, or other material. Goes into a horse's mouth.

BITLESS: Riding a horse without a bit in the mouth. This includes riding in a halter, hackamore, bosal, or side pull.

BOSAL: A Western bitless bridle that has a braided rawhide noseband used in Western riding, trail riding, and on younger horses; works by applying pressure on the bridge of the nose and bars of the jaw.

BREAST COLLAR AND BREASTPLATE: A piece of leather or other material that sits across the front of the horse's chest and connects to the saddle or harness to keep either from sliding back.

BRIDLE: The piece of equipment that goes on the head of a horse used to control him as you ride.

BUCK: An action where the horse lowers its head and jumps upward, arching his back and rapidly kicking his hind feet into the air.

CANTER: A three-beat gait faster than a trot and slower than a gallop. Term used in English riding and is called lope when riding Western.

CANTLE: Part of the saddle, both English and Western, behind the rider. It is the back ridge of a saddle.

CAVESSON: A part of an English bridle that consists of a noseband and headstall and sits on the nose under the larger headstall.

CRYPTORCHID: When one or both testicles (testes) are not descended in the scrotum, the horse is called a ridgling, rig, or cryptorchid. Cryptorchidism is a developmental defect in both animals and humans.

CINCH: The strap (may be leather, fabric, rope, neoprene, or other material) that is used to secure the Western saddle on a horse. The English equivalent is a girth.

CLICKER TRAINING: A method of training using positive reinforcement and bridging stimulus to get desired results. Horses learn to recognize a clicking sound from a small device as a signal they have performed correctly before getting a reward.

143

COLIC: Acute pain in a horse's abdomen, ranging from mild to life-threateningly severe, it may include intestinal displacement or blockage. The leading cause of death among domesticated horses.

COLLECTED, COLLECTION: A horse carrying himself in a balanced manner using his hindquarters more than his forequarters.

COLT: Intact (not castrated) male horse under the age of three years.

CONDITIONED RESPONSE: When a horse is trained to a stimulus the same way every time he confronts that stimulus.

CONFORMATION: The physical structure of the horse; how he is put together.

DESENSITIZE: To expose a horse to a frightening stimulus repeatedly until he no longer responds.

FAR SIDE: The right side of the horse.

FARRIER: Usually, but not always, a blacksmith who shoes horses. Many farriers specialize in barefoot horses that are not regularly shod.

FILLY: Female horse under the age of four years.

FLOAT: The rasping the sharp points of a horse's teeth to maintain level surfaces on each tooth. Floating allows the horse to chew and utilize his food better.

FOAL: A young horse, regardless of gender, under the age of one year. A mare "foals" when giving birth.

FROG: Triangular in shape, it extends midway from the heels toward the toe. Touching the ground, it acts like a pump to send blood back up the leg with each step.

GAITS: The different ways in which a horse travels, including walk, trot, canter, and gallop.

GALLOP: The fastest a horse runs; faster than a lope or canter and is a three-beat gait.

GELDING: Neutered or castrated male horse of any age.

GIRTH: The strap (may be leather, fabric, rope, neoprene, or other material) that is used to secure the English saddle on a horse. The Western equivalent is a cinch.

GRADE: A horse with unknown bloodlines; not registered and is not able to be registered due to unknown origin.

GROOM: A person, usually employee, who looks after horses. To clean horses is to groom them.

GYMKHANA: An equestrian event consisting of speed pattern racing and timed games for riders on horses.

HALTER: Also called a head collar; headgear that is used to lead a horse and is made of nylon, leather, rope, or other material.

HAND: One hand equals four inches. (A 15-hand horse is 60 inches tall at the highest point of the withers).

HOOF PICK: A metal device used to clean horses' hooves.

IRON: The English term for stirrup; metal pieces that attach to the saddle using leather straps; it is where a rider rests his feet.

KICK: Horse lashes out with his back leg or legs.

LATIGO: Strap made of leather, nylon or other soft material that is attached to a metal ring on a saddle tree, used to attach a cinch to a Western saddle.

LEAD ROPE: Used to lead a horse from the ground, it attaches to the halter. Made of cotton, nylon, or other synthetic material.

LOPE: A three-beat gait faster than a trot and slower than a gallop. Term used in riding Western and is called canter when riding English.

LUNGE LINE: Longe Line. A thirty-foot long rope or flat nylon or cotton line used to lunge a horse.

LUNGE: Ground work consisting of sending a horse around a stationary person in all gaits to teach good ground manners and to exercise the animal from the ground.

MARE: Adult female horse over the age of four years.

MUCKING: To clean the stable of wet and soiled bedding and to remove all manure.

NAVICULAR DISEASE: Changes in the navicular bone, usually where the deep flexor tendon passes over the bone. Causes pain and lameness. No long-term cure as it is generally a degenerative disease.

NEAR SIDE: The left side of the horse.

NOSEBANDS—Flash Figure 8, and Drop

OXBOW STIRRUP: A wooden stirrup resembling an oxbow in shape and having a rounded bottom where the rider's foot rests. Used for riding bucking horses as the rider's foot can be put through to the heel.

PAW: The action of a horse when he strikes forward with a front leg or hoof as though digging.

POMMEL: The front most portion of the saddle.

REAR: The action of a horse lifting both front legs off the ground.

SIDE PULL: A type of bridle that has no bit and works by applying pressure to the top of the nose and under the bars of the jaw.

SNAFFLE (BIT): Type of bit that can have a jointed or straight mouthpiece, but does not ever have shanks. Each rein works independently and the bit applies pressure to the bars of the mouth and tongue.

SPURS: Artificial aid, made of metal. This device is strapped onto a rider's heel and is used to apply focused pressure on horse's side by use of a small spike or spiked wheel called a rowel—used in both English and Western riding and comes in a wide range of look and severity.

STALLION: Intact male horse over the age of three years capable of breeding mares.

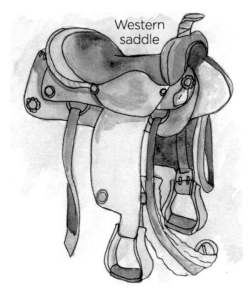

Western saddle

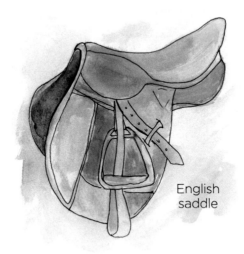

English saddle

STIRRUP: Western term for Iron, where the rider's foot rests while riding.

STRIKE: The action of a horse pawing high and fast with one front leg. Usually a precursor to initiating a fight between horses; mares will strike at stallions when not in heat.

TACK: The equipment used with horses, including bridles, saddles, halters, etc.

TACKING UP: To saddle and bridle a horse.

TETANUS: Serious bacterial infection caused by Clostridium tetani, which enters the body through puncture wounds. Also called lockjaw.

THRUSH: Fungal or bacterial infection of the bottom of the hoof at the frog. Thrush is typified by rank-smelling discharge from the cleft of the frog.

TROT: A two-beat diagonal gait that is faster than a walk and slower than a canter or lope.

WALK: A four-beat gait that is the slowest gait.

WHIP: Any device that is used to hit a horse. Crop is another word for a short whip. Also Whip can mean the driver of a carriage.

WITHERS: The highest point at the base of the neck and above the shoulders where a horse is measured. It is just in front of where the saddle sits.

ACKNOWLEDGMENTS

Thank you never seems enough so I hope you each know how large of a part you've played in helping me to write and publish this book.

Thank you, Roger, for doing all you've done to make this happen and never once complaining. Thank you to all of my clients—both horse and human; without you, I never could know the things that have pointed me in the right direction to write how best to help you. Thank you to my friend and illustrator, Jennipher Cunningham for creating the exact right images and injecting the best colours and energy, and who always got the arts to me in time for whatever deadline I was up against. My friend and editor, Tom Locke, who fixed all my silly mistakes and guided me to the finish line with kindness every step of the way. Thank you, to my friend and graphic artist, Jenny Hancey, who designed the vague vision and made it real, while cheerfully putting up with my crazy ideas and consistently smiling every single day. A special thanks to my friend Beck McEwen for our conversations while riding that allowed me to see what this project could look like right from the start; even though I had no clue at the time. Thank you to all who were Beta Readers on call and encouraged me when I floundered. And lastly, I thank my dogs, Hana, Maggie and Norman, who tirelessly and enthusiastically listened as I read the manuscript to them while we paced through the house, across the yard and down to the barn. Even now, as I read this to them, they anxiously and enthusiastically await the treat they know will follow.

To each of you, a hug and a huge thank you, for without you, this would not be a 'thing'.

–Tanya

About the Author

Tanya Buck grew up with horses, which is what everyone who writes a book on horses says, but Tanya's experience was anything but traditional. Her early childhood in Carmel, California, was spent working on her parents' ranch—training, guiding trail rides, teaching others to ride, mucking stalls and running the front end of the horse rental business. She began riding before she could walk and was starting young horses and fixing problems with others by age eight. She competed in her first open horse show about this same time and showed both English and Western as a junior rider throughout California. She competed in the 1973 Olympic Trials at the Pebble Beach Equestrian Center when she was fifteen.

When she was sixteen, both parents died and she found herself on her own, happy she could earn a living teaching and training. Happy for the work, she took on all horses with any problem, teaching them to trust humans, and it was from these animals that Tanya gained her own horse sense. She became a more empathetic and sympathetic trainer and instructor specializing in equine trauma recovery. Her philosophy of keeping both horse and rider feeling safe was born during this time as it became clear that feeling safe was the key to unlocking the door to both humans and horses progressing quickly and easily.

Tanya is UC Davis Certified as a breeding manager, is a certified 4-H judge, an open horse show judge, and taught 4-H for eleven years. She was a Pony Club Instructor for five years and has owned and operated her own holistic horse training business for over 40 years. She is actively involved with horse rescue nationwide and is on the board of Happy Endings Animal Rescue and Sanctuary in Solvang, California. She is involved in the Colorado Horse Rescue Network, saving horses that might otherwise be shipped to slaughter. She is an active member of Front Range Animal Evacuation Team in Colorado to help facilitate the evacuation of horses and other animals in times of emergency.

She is a published author (*White Horse, A Novel*) and has judged writing contests sponsored by Rocky Mountain Fiction Writers, Pikes Peak Writers, and Northern Colorado Writers.

She graduated from University California, Davis, where she majored in Animal Science with a minor in English before moving to the mountains of Colorado. She has been married for eleven years to her husband, Roger, and they live in the Rocky Mountains with a few dogs, cats, birds, and of course, horses. Other than riding and teaching, Tanya loves photography, reading, writing, hiking, snowshoeing, and scuba diving.

Tanya is a member of Citizens Against Equine Slaughter, WWW (Women Writing the West), FRAET (Front Range Animal Evacuation Team), and DAN (Divers Alert network).

Currently, Tanya presents the message of this book during seminars and clinics she teaches.

Thank you for reading and sharing! Reviews are welcomed at Amazon.com.

Inquires are welcome and should be sent to:
Tanya Buck
Flying Frog Publications
info@TanyaBuck.com
www.TanyaBuck.com

Notes

Made in United States
North Haven, CT
19 December 2024